A SECOND CHANCE

Clementino Armada Dumdum Jr
Mark Anthony A. Buccat

By Clementino Armada Dumdum Jr, Mark Anthony A. Buccat

ISBN:

Hardbound-978-621-470-586-3

MOBI/KINDLE -978-621-470-587-0

Softbound/Paperback -978-621-470-588-7

Published by:
Poetry Planet Book Publishing House
Rosario, Pozorrubio, Pangasinan, Philippines
Contact Number: 09554960094
Email: maritesritumalta@gmail.com

PREFACE

As a social work professional with years of experience working with children in conflict with the law, we have witnessed firsthand the devastating effects of juvenile delinquency. Despite various intervention programs developed by different agencies and the government's efforts to reduce this behavior, the number of cases has continued to rise. The Philippines, in particular, has seen a skyrocketing number of Filipino children in conflict with the law, with thousands of children being arrested and detained each year.

Throughout our career, we have come to realize that a child's environment, including their family and community, plays a significant role in their behavior. We strongly believe that a series of activities, such as counseling, skills training, education, and other activities that may enhance a child's psychological, emotional, and psycho-social well-being, may address the issues that could cause a child to commit an offense. However, the family is the most critical factor in helping the child towards transformation. When families cannot provide care, love, and guidance during the turbulent years of adolescence, peer groups become the source of support and a sense of belonging.

As part of the Manila Youth Reception Center (MYRC) and a Social Work Professor, we have encountered challenges in helping these children due to their unfortunate situation. MYRC has provided guidance and opportunities that are significant in enabling children to overcome their struggles and have a "second chance" in life. However, MYRC does not have concrete programs and services to help children in conflict with the law in their transformational change. The MYRC management is currently developing a comprehensive package of programs and services aimed at addressing the immediate needs of the children in conflict with the law, the speedy disposition of their cases, and their spiritual, behavioral, cognitive, and transformational change.

Despite RA 10630 taking effect on November 7, 2013, gaps or challenges still exist in implementing the amended Act. The first challenge is the lack of compliance with various provisions of the law. In this book, we aim to explore the various theories behind high rates of juvenile delinquency, provide a means of understanding this behavior, and create a platform for developing better intervention measures. We share our experiences at MYRC, the challenges that we have encountered, and the solutions that the management is developing.

We also discuss the importance of compliance with various provisions of the law to effectively address juvenile delinquency.

Together, we believe we can create a more just society that promotes health, safety, justice, and equity, where a better world is indeed possible for children in conflict with the law. Their journey is like the air we breathe. They are embedded in our institutions, structures, and norms. Indeed, most of the time, we are even hardly aware of them, much less the way they shape our experience and our understanding of our experiences. We hope that this book will inspire change and encourage action towards a better future for all.

TABLE OF CONTENTS

Chapter I

THE PROBLEM AND ITS SETTING

Introduction

I believe a series of activities may address issues that could cause a child to commit an offense. These activities may take the form of an individualized treatment program, such as counseling, skills training, education, and other activities that may enhance a child's psychological/emotional and psycho-social well-being.

Juvenile delinquency has been a major problem affecting modern day societies. It is an antisocial, criminal or illegal behavior and acts that have become common among children and adolescents. Recently, many theories have been formulated to explain the reasons behind high rates of juvenile delinquency. Various agencies have developed different intervention programs to reduce this behavior. A combination of these theories and programs has provided a means of understanding this behavior and a platform for developing better intervention measures. Social guidance and counseling of juvenile offenders is the most effective means of reducing juvenile delinquency, as opposed to the use of punishment (Mendel, 2002).

Cases of juvenile delinquency have been on the rise despite increased government efforts to reduce them. There has been a controversy over how to handle juvenile offenders, with some people arguing that they should be treated like adult offenders. The government has considered both public safety and the need to rehabilitate the juvenile offenders in its effort to fight this behavior. However, this has not been effective in reducing the cases of juvenile delinquency. All over the world, an examination of the juvenile justice system is being done. Among the areas of concern undergoing re-investigation is the philosophy of punishment involving juvenile offenders and bringing them into the juvenile system of justice.

In the Philippines, the number of Filipino children in conflict with the law is skyrocketing. According to the Juvenile Justice Network, thousands of children are being arrested and detained each year. Most of these detained children in jails are mixed with notorious adult criminals; the boys are abused and the girls are raped. The distinctive effects which delinquency engenders on the child, his family and the community in which he lives have increasingly been felt as the Philippine socio-cultural, economic and political systems have been transformed.

I've been part of the Manila Youth Reception Center (MYRC) since February 2006. I have handled several cases of children in conflict with the law. It's been a tough job because some children are not visited by their parents; hence, the need to conduct house visitation to validate the reason for their absence. Some children don't have families, and they are not residents of Manila; so, I need to refer them to other NGOs. I believe the family is the most important factor in helping the child towards transformation, but because of their unfortunate situation, it's been difficult for me to apply a generalist intervention approach.

When families cannot provide care, love and guidance during the turbulent years of adolescence, peer group becomes the source of support and sense of belonging. However, the guidance and opportunities provided by MYRC are significant in enabling children to hurdle their struggles in order to have a "second chance" in life. There are flaws in the juvenile justice system coupled with shortcomings in terms of services and staff; but these challenges are being addressed in the best way possible. The greater challenge is the reintegration of the children with their families and communities. I believe they had built the foundation and preparation for transformation through the various psychosocial interventions and other services provided.

To date, MYRC does not have concrete programs and services to help CICLs in their transformational change. Since MYRC was established when juvenile delinquency was not rampant, and transformational change was more of a concern for parents and teachers, it was not included as part of the institution's intervention.

The MYRC management is developing a comprehensive package of programs and services aimed at addressing not only the immediate needs of the CICLs, the speedy disposition of their cases, but also to focus on their spiritual, behavioral, cognitive and transformational change. Thus, there is a need for additional human resources, specifically a resident psychologist, a recreation specialist, group workers, skills trainer, and a spiritual adviser. The specific important functions of a resident psychologist would be to administer psychological evaluation and address the cognitive and behavioral concerns of the CICLs. The group workers could facilitate group dynamics and other group work activities. The recreation specialist could facilitate worthwhile recreational activities for CICLs. The skills trainer will educate CICLs and help them develop a skill set which they could use once released from the center. The spiritual adviser could provide pieces of advice and counseling for their spiritual needs. These are being raised to the department head for action. Further, the management is also working on continuously developing the knowledge, skills and behavior of the employees in the center, especially the household attendants because they are the primary caregivers of the CICLs in the center. Lack of conducive facilities for CICLs was also raised to the department head.

I believe a better world is indeed possible for Children in Conflict with the Law (CICL) and can create a more just society that promotes health, safety, justice and equity. Their journey is like the air we breathe. They are embedded in our institutions, structures, and norms. Indeed, most of the time, we are even hardly aware of them; much less the way they shape our experience and our understanding of our experiences.

After RA 9344 was amended, RA 10630 took effect on November 7, 2013. It can be said the juvenile system is in place, and all legal bases are laid down. However, gaps or challenges still exist in implementing the amended Act.

The first challenge is lack of compliance with various provisions of the law. In particular, the provided mandates and duties of LGUs are still not fully observed. It is recognized that the success of the law lies in the proactive involvement of local government units, starting from the level of the barangay up to the provincial government.

Second, the detention of children pending trial is still reported to be prevalent. Children are continually committed by Family Courts or Regional Trial Courts to BJMP-managed jails and worse, to the national penitentiary, where they encounter overcrowded and in poor condition facilities. In addition, the lack of specialized courts, facilities, and personnel and conflicting provisions is a significant issue. For example, the Supreme Court Revised Rule on Children in Conflict with the Law allows children charged with non-serious offenses to be placed under the care of a jail if there are no youth facilities available in their jurisdiction.

They also needed public support for the steadfast implementation of the law. Unfortunately, public misconceptions about the Act still prevail. There is skepticism about the efficacy of the Act, especially its inability to prevent recidivism among CICL.

Finally, there are many NGO-managed Youth Homes/BPAs that are still not accredited by DSWD. According to the DSWD submission, there are only four accredited BPAs, as of the end of 2014. While we rarely think of worldview and the shaping of their narratives as power, changing a structure or system requires many people to have the collective belief that those changes are necessary and possible. Expanding and influencing public consciousness toward change and shaping their narrative, then it will become an important form of wisdom to enhance our delivery of service.

The process of this study leads to my personal transformation because our worldviews are often linked to unexamined assumptions about the experiences and journey of the children in conflict with the law. These assumptions, unchecked, become so entrenched that they feel like "common sense," or self-evident truths. Unmasking the narrative is difficult, or even jarring, but it can also deepen relationships among the people — and organizations — that undertake it together because it is based on sharing experiences of children in conflict with the law.

General Background of the Study

A. Global Context

Millions of children around the world suffer harm from crime and abuse of power. They come into contact with justice systems as victims, witnesses or alleged offenders, and for care, custody or protection.

Established by a 1997 Resolution of the Economic and Social Council, the Inter-Agency Coordination Panel on Juvenile Justice, (formerly known as the UN Coordination Panel on Technical Advice and Assistance in Juvenile Justice or the UNCPJJ) aims to coordinate policies, projects and activities among international organizations engaged with national authorities in juvenile justice reform. The work of the Panel is guided by the relevant provisions of the Convention on the Rights of the Child, other relevant international standards related to juvenile justice, and the recommendations of the UN Committee on the Rights of the Child.

The aim of this body is to enhance national and global coordination in juvenile justice by identifying Panel member organizations working at country level and their activities. It further aims to encourage respective field offices to work together towards a common approach at country level, and promote ongoing dialogue with national partners in juvenile justice reform. They also identify, develop and disseminate common tools and good practices and always bring protection of the rights of children in conflict with the law on to agenda of the international community.

In several countries worldwide, member organizations of the Panel have supported coordination for implementing the recommendations of the Committee on the Rights of the Child. In 2000, Uganda, where coordination made possible a training and strategy development workshop, was organized by OHCHR, DCI, UNICEF, Save the Children-UK and Danida. Beginning 2003, Uruguay, where DCI, OMCT, Save the Children, Terre des Hommes Foundation, UNICEF and others collaborated to conduct monitoring and high-level advocacy activities. In 2004, the Panel undertook a global mapping of justice initiatives for children in conflict with the law in 127 countries, an approximate breakdown of the panel members' organizational activities in juvenile justice reform, dated March 2004.

The Panel now has a shared website, accessible to all staff of member organizations. Future initiatives of the Panel include the establishment of a focal point and secretariat for the Panel, the establishment of a public website and coordinated technical support for the production and dissemination of the CRC Committee's upcoming General Comment on Juvenile Justice.

The decline in arrests of juveniles continued through 2019 estimates based on data from the FBI's Uniform Crime Reporting Program, highlight trends in juvenile arrests. After falling 67% since 2006, the number of juvenile arrests reached a new low in 2019. The number of juvenile arrests for violent crime offenses was cut in half between 2006 and 2019. By 2019, arrest rates for violent crimes fell substantially from the 1994 peak for every age group younger than 45. Youth under age 15 and females each accounted for about a third of juvenile arrests in 2019. Juvenile arrests for Property Crime Index offenses fell 73% between 2008 and 2019. This publication was prepared by Charles Puzzanchera, National Center for Juvenile Justice, with funds provided by OJJDP in November 2020 Analysis of Federal Bureau of Investigation arrest data from the Bureau of Justice Statistics (data years 1980–2014) and the National Center for Juvenile Justice (data years 2015–2019).

UNICEF estimates that over one million children worldwide are deprived of their liberty by law enforcement officials. This is likely to be a significant underestimate given the difficulties in obtaining data about the many overlooked and unreported children in custody.

Most children in detention–around 59 percent–have not been tried and sentenced. Only a minority of these children eventually receive a custodial sentence, suggesting that pre-trial detention is regularly used as a sanction, in violation of the right to be innocent until proven guilty. Children's cases are often processed through justice systems designed for adults that are not adapted to children's rights and specific needs.

Conditions of detention are substandard, overcrowded, and deny children their rights, such as the right to standards of health and education. Children are regularly mixed with adults, increasing the risk of violence, abuse, and exploitation. As a result, detention rarely results in the child's rehabilitation and reintegration into society, which should be the aim of any justice intervention in line with the Convention on the Rights of the Child.

Convention on the Rights of the Child prohibits the death penalty or sentences of life imprisonment without possibility of release for children. Child victims and witnesses of crime are often re-victimized by justice systems that are not adapted to their rights and needs. Professionals–including the police, prosecutors and judges–often lack specialized training in dealing with child victims and witnesses. Related procedures are rarely child-sensitive.

The National Criminal Justice and Public Health Alliance created Transformational Criminal Justice Narrative, a toolkit that support community organizers and health equity advocates in developing, using, and adapting transformational narratives to advance equity in the criminal and juvenile justice systems. The National Criminal Justice and Public Health Alliance's Narrative Workgroup went through a process to develop a transformational narrative. I found that the process to be incredibly eye opening — it sharpened their analysis, changed how they communicate about their work, strengthened their relationships and deepened their resolve to transform the system.

After completing their process and sharing the transformational narrative with others, they realized the process was as important as the product, and they helped others go through a similar process. This toolkit includes the following materials - an introduction to public narratives and their role in community organizing, systems change, and public policy change, a six-step guide to developing a transformational narrative, and a set of exercises and tips to support transformational narrative development

B. Asian context

Children can be in contact with the justice system as a victim, witness or offender. Yet the justice system is often structured to deal with adults, not allowing the space for the child to participate. A child, particularly as a victim, requires additional safeguards to understand the proceedings. If the child is an alleged or convicted perpetrator, the balance between the punishment and the rehabilitation must lean towards rehabilitation. In South Asia, the focus is on punishment, with countries in the region permitting physical and corporal punishment, as well as long-term detention, with few options for diversion or alternatives to detention.

In breach of the principle that the deprivation of liberty be used only as a measure of last resort and for the shortest appropriate period, deprivation of liberty remains a common form of punishment for juvenile offenders, who are often detained for several years and, sometimes, for indeterminate periods of time.

They also detained children in immigration, mental health or for their own 'protection'. While decisions taken to detain a child administratively may vary in terms of context, rationale and legal framework, it is common that the decision is taken not by a judge or a court, but by another body or a professional who is not independent of the executive branch of government.

Children victims of trafficking and sexual exploitation are often treated as offenders rather than victims and are often detained together with those who have committed an offense. In South Asia, the arrest and detention of children living and working on the streets by police officers on grounds such as vagrancy, indecent behaviour or prostitution, being a public nuisance or exposed to moral danger, is reported to occur in Bangladesh, Nepal, Pakistan and Sri Lanka.

Most children in detention have not committed serious offenses. A significant number have not even committed a criminal offence and are deprived of their liberty for a 'status offence' such as dropping out of school, getting married, running away from home and alcohol use. Status offenses are not considered criminal offenses when committed by adults.

Child victims' access to justice is often impeded by obstacles such as lack of knowledge about their rights, court and legal representation fees and dependence on adults to bring rights violations to justice. Children may also be in contact with the judicial system in cases of civil or family law, such as custody, divorce hearings, witnesses to domestic violence, placement in alternative care. Often, like in criminal proceedings, they are not heard.

Setting the minimum age of criminal responsibility too low also has a detrimental effect on children. Except for Afghanistan and Bhutan, the minimum age of criminal responsibility in South Asian countries is below international standards, ranging from 7 (Pakistan, India), 8 (Sri Lanka), 9 (Bangladesh), 10 (Maldives, Nepal), to 12 (Afghanistan, Bhutan).

The East Asia and Pacific region contains over one-quarter of the world's children - around 580 million children in total. Because of a child's age and still developing maturity, they are highly vulnerable and require special measures to protect them when in contact with the justice system. Yet, in some Southeast Asia countries, children are treated like adults under the law and the justice system cannot consider their needs and best interests or to address the root causes that brought them into conflict with the law.

"Preventing violence against children in justice systems forms a key component of UNODC's work in Justice for Children," said Mr. Jeremy Douglas, UNODC Regional Representative for Southeast Asia and the Pacific. Mr. Douglas was speaking in Bangkok as a keynote speaker at a workshop on Responding to Violence against Children in contact with the Justice System. Organized by UNODC in partnership with UNICEF and the Thailand Institute of Justice, the three-day regional training workshop sought to enhance the skills and knowledge of 150 taking part criminal justice professionals - police officers, prosecutors, judges, social workers and academics - from 16 East Asia and Pacific countries. Aside from these, there have been several UN instruments adopted through the years, such as the Beijing Rules and others, which serve as policy framework standards for juvenile justice.

Other keynote speakers included HRH Princess Bajrakitiyabha Mahidol of Thailand, and Mr. Daniel Poole, UNICEF Regional Director for East Asia and the Pacific, who both delivered speeches that highlighted the importance of a functioning child–friendly justice system that will ensure that all children have access to, and are better served and protected by national justice systems. The workshop was the first capacity building initiative of its kind to pilot-test two new UNODC tools related to the recently approved UN international instrument–'The United Nations Model Strategies and Practical Measures on the Elimination of Violence against Children in the Field of Crime Prevention and Criminal Justice'. The adoption of this instrument by the General Assembly of the United Nations in December 2014 means that UNODC will have a new benchmark for action to identify the needs and capacities of countries and to provide technical assistance and advisory services to prevent and respond to violence against children.

Participants from the 16 countries identified four priority strategies, which included promoting research and data collection, establishing effective detection and reporting mechanisms for violence against children, strengthening the capacity of justice professionals and enhancing cooperation among various sectors to prevent and respond to violence against children. At the workshop, UNODC lead trainer and 'curriculum writer, Dr. Geeta Sekhon, pilot tested a new UNODC/UNICEF training curriculum on how to treat child victims and witnesses. In stressing the vulnerability of children in contact with the justice system and their need for special protection, trainees were encouraged to share real case examples and jointly provide practical solutions on how children should be treated.

The training method, with the key objective to enhance the skills and knowledge of the participating police officers, prosecutors, judges and social workers–comprised a wide range of lectures, games, exercises, role plays, case studies and group discussions facilitated by Justice for Children experts from UNODC and UNICEF.

Participants pledged to become agents of change when dealing with child victims and witnesses to crime. The pledge, inspired by Yasmeen Shariff, member of the UN Committee on the Rights of the Child, was taken at the end of the three-day regional training workshop.

C. National Context

In the Philippines, the advocacy for passaging a juvenile justice law was intensified after the release of the UN Committee on the Rights of the Child's concluding observations on the Philippine's Initial Report in 1995. Since then, various bills on juvenile justice were filed in both houses of Congress and government agencies. Non-governmental organizations (NGOs) and child rights advocates conducted campaigns for the enactment of the proposed measure. Juvenile Justice and Welfare Act (JJWA, or the Act), also known as Republic Act (RA) 9344, was enacted after more than a decade of advocacy and collaboration among government agencies, NGOs, faith-based organizations, and child rights advocates. The enactment of the JJWA provided for a comprehensive and child sensitive juvenile justice and welfare system. The Act adopted the concept of restorative justice in the crafting of policies and implementing the programs relating to CICL and tried to provide a holistic approach to preventing juvenile delinquency.

The salient features of RA 9344 include increasing the minimum age of criminal responsibility for over nine to over 15 years of age; establishment and strengthening of local councils for protecting children; establishment of comprehensive juvenile intervention programs; establishment of community-based programs on juvenile justice and welfare; establishment and implementation of community diversion programs; provision on status offenses, so any conduct not considered an offense or not penalized if committed by an adult shall not be considered an offense and shall not be punished if committed by a child; provision for child-sensitive proceedings; and imposition of disposition measures.

Under these laws, the Juvenile Justice and Welfare Council (JJWC) was created and mandated to oversee the implementation of additional features of the juvenile justice system, one of which was the introduction of the concept of restorative justice and diversion. Under this new juvenile justice system, the existing government-run, center-based rehabilitation programs were further strengthened and several community-based diversion programs were instituted for the social integration of children in conflict with the law (CICL). These interventions include, but are not limited to: (1) the Regional Rehabilitation Centers for Youth (RRCY) operated by DSWD, (2) the Bahay Pag-asa (BPA) facilities established by local government units (LGUs), and (3) community-based diversion programs.

The social worker manages over-all operations of the facility. He/She handles the orientation of DSWD child protection policy and management of CICL cases under R.A. 9344, as amended. The social worker is also responsible for facilitating training on behavior management and on various therapy models applicable to CICL cases.

One of DSWD's primary responsibilities, as the Chair and as a member of the JJWC, an inter-agency body tasked to coordinate the implementation of juvenile intervention programs in the country, is to establish and maintain the Regional Rehabilitation Centers for Youth (RRCY).

RRCY is a 24-hour residential center for the rehabilitation of youth offenders below 18 years of age, whose sentences have been suspended. It also serves as a nurturing out-of-home placement for children in need of rehabilitation. Several RRCY were already in existence before the enactment of JJWA.

UNICEF began helping the Philippines in 1948. The juvenile justice reform in the Philippines is in line with UNICEF's focus on global juvenile justice programming, which emphasizes the reduction of the number of children held in police custody, pre-trial detention, prisons, and juvenile rehabilitation centers. The role of UNICEF Philippines has been to support the drafting off, and advocacy for passaging RA 9344, and to assist government–run centers for CICL by offering capacity building activities to social workers and center authorities, and providing supplies for technical and vocational skills training, and as other recreational activities for the children.

As is the situation in other parts of the world, there have been debates on the efficacy of the current juvenile justice system to prevent re–offending and recidivism among CICL in the

Philippines. However, no studies have, so far, shed light on the effects of this rehabilitation and intervention programs. Also, timely research needs to be conducted on implementing existing diversion programs to identify effective diversion models. Against this background, UNICEF commissioned an independent evaluation to assess how center-based rehabilitation and diversion programs contribute to the overall objectives of juvenile justice and welfare administration in the Philippines.

All programs are relevant in meeting the needs of CICL in the areas of health care, education, skills, security and safety, and spiritual and value formation. They are also relevant to the aim of bringing Philippine juvenile justice law and practice into compliance with international conventions. Two salient examples are provision of the principal and procedures for diversion, and the minimum age of criminal responsibility (MACR). These programs also contribute to the overall national justice and welfare reform by creating a child-friendly juvenile justice system. The residential and diversion programs under this evaluation have clearly reflected the human rights-based approach to development.

However, significant gaps still exist in meeting international conventions' rights protection standards. The full implementation of the Law, especially the diversion programs, and adequate compliance at the local level are not satisfactory. All these realities take place against the backdrop of a shift in the focus of UNICEF from an issue-based to a system-based approach. A serious challenge confronting the programs under this evaluation is how to further establish their relevance to the overall child protection strategies at the local level and sustain the attention of major international technical help providers.

Most programs provide an enabling environment for the rehabilitation and reintegration of CICL. Through these programs, a large proportion of children are being diverted out of the formal criminal justice system, which inevitably avoids the negative social and psychological impacts of labeling these children as "criminals." Most CICL can continue their formal education schooling through the programs in which they take part. Some CICL can attend vocational training programs. Interviews with parents and children confirm changes in the behavior of the CICL in the programs.

Several factors are identified as negatively affecting the rehabilitation and reintegration of CICL significantly, which can turn into facilitating factors if handled properly. They include: (1) delayed court proceedings, which has resulted in the prolonged stay of CICL in detention institutions or other facilities before they are officially admitted into the rehabilitation, intervention, or diversion programs, (2) lack of implementation of required customized interventions for CICL, which has limited the effectiveness of the programs, (3) insufficient capacity of juvenile justice actors, e.g. social workers, police, prosecutors, and judges, and (4) weak commitment from the LGU, which has significantly affected the implementation of programs for CICL at the local level.

The DSWD has a limited influence on the programs operated by LGUs and NGOs. It does not provide direct financial support to these programs. The regional offices of the DSWD play an important role in coordinating the capacity-building activities once new guidelines relating to CICL are issued. The DSWD regional offices and training recipients, comprising staff from LGUs and NGO-run programs, have noticed inadequacy in the frequency and depth of these trainings. The accreditation of NGOs and LGUs by the DSWD is a clear avenue of influence. Other avenues for the DSWD to exert its influence can be found in the different councils, such as the Regional Juvenile Justice and Welfare Committees (RJJWC) that are mandated to ensure the effective implementation of the laws and coordination among their member agencies. By May 2015, 11 RJJWC have already convened their members and 14 RJJWCs have already hired and set-up their permanent secretariat.

Although UNICEF does not maintain a direct relationship with the programs under evaluation, the agency provides technical help and capacity-building for the DSWD, and even material equipment, sometimes. UNICEF also attends meetings of different networks and provides technical advice. This type of technical help is much valued by the stakeholders because it brings more effectiveness, as opposed to simply providing funding.

RRCYs are better funded, compared to other programs because of stable support from the DSWD. The funding for BPAs mainly comes from the LGU budget, while NGO-run programs depend heavily on donations. Due to low compliance at the local level, the number of BPAs and community-based programs is still not enough. On the ground, the team found out that some RRCYs and BPAs have established an agreement to host CICL on a cost-sharing basis.

In almost all the programs, social workers are also tasked with handling issues that are not related to CICL. For example, in community-based programs, social workers who are LGU employees handle all categories of social welfare; therefore, they cannot spend enough time on the diversion program. Almost all program staff, regardless of their job title as social workers or house parents, stated that lacking training affects their efficiency at work.

Financial resources, like human resources, are quite stretched in the programs. To augment their financial resources, the various programs do their own resource mobilization by tapping the private sector, NGOs, or religious organizations. Typically, centers receive donations in cash or in kind from these groups. Sometimes, these groups sponsor specific CICL activities. Some facilities also implement income-generating activities (e.g. selling the products of the CICL) or various kinds of resource mobilization in cooperation with the communities they serve.

Existing research shows that if the government focuses on strengthening the community-based diversion programs under the barangays of a municipality or city, cost-efficiency will be promoted. The primary goal of the Law on local intervention and rehabilitation will be achieved.

BPAs and NGO-run facilities are facing more sustainability challenges than the RRCYs. At the local level, with the amendment of the JJWA, the responsibility of LGUs has been further clarified. Today, of the 81 provinces, 15 have been able to establish a BPA in partnership with the DSWD or the JJWC. As for highly urbanized cities, only a handful has complied with Section 49 of RA 10630. The accountability system at the local government level determines whether the budget items given to CICL will be adequately considered; and whether both the skills and the workload of local social workers and house parents can be maintained at a reasonable level. The stability of staff at the regional level (e.g. staff working in the programs and other duty-bearers) requires that people with proper training on CICL stay in their positions for an extended period to avoid frequent turnover or re-assignment.

At the national level, the legal framework is already in place. However, the sustainability of the programs under evaluation depends on the reforms in the justice system and the social welfare system. For effective reintegration, there is a need to prepare the CICL and the community, especially the family, to support the children and the parents after the discharge of the CICL from the programs. The long-term sustainability of these programs also depends on the correct understanding of their intervention approach. As clearly provided in JJWA and its amendment, institutionalization should be the last resort for CICL. Implementation of programs which aim to prevent children from coming into CICL is more cost efficient than maintaining and operating rehabilitation and diversion programs.

Capacity Building: In order to deliver efficiently the services required by the Act and its amendment through a multi-agency approach, training for duty-bearers, member agencies of the JJWC, and coordinating agencies have been continuously conducted since 2006. The JJWA also mandated the capacity building of the relevant State agencies. Here are a few examples: The DSWD implemented a training program for their social workers to upgrade their skills. The Commission on Human Rights and the Department of Justice included the discussions of the Act in its investigators and prosecutors' training, respectively. The JJWC, in partnership with the Bureau of Corrections, the Board of Pardon and Parole, the National Youth Commission, the National Federation of *Sangguniang Kabataan*, the Philippine National Police (PNP), the Bureau of Jail Management and Penology (BJMP), and the Department of Interior and Local Government (DILG), funded and organized island wide/regional trainings for the agencies' focal persons.

To increase public awareness, the JJWC sponsored a radio program aired in 2013, featuring salient provisions of the Act and pertinent information on how to handle CICL cases. The agency is currently gathering and collecting data and working on the establishment of a national information system. In 2012, the JJWC launched the localization of the Comprehensive National Juvenile Intervention Program (CNJIP), also called the Comprehensive Local Juvenile Intervention Program

(CLJIP). Seven selected Local Government Units are being trained and provided with technical help in the conceptualization and implementation of their own programs.

RA 9344 mandates that two of JJWC members should be NGO representatives to institutionalize the partnership with civil society. In its latest Strategic Planning (2015-2017), the JJWC further stated that all its member agencies, including 12 government agencies and two NGO representatives, took part in the planning, drafting, and finalization of the document. NGOs have been actively involved in the policy formulation and direction setting in the juvenile justice sector, which is led by government agencies and coordinating agencies of the JJWC. The JJWC, through its NGO representatives, maintains working relationships with juvenile justice advocates and networks.

The establishment of an Intensive Juvenile Intervention and Support Center (IJISC) for CICL who are under the minimum age of criminal responsibility in 'Bahay Pag-asa' is one of the key enhancements in the law.

Under the law, the 'Bahay Pag-asa' is managed by a multi-disciplinary team composed of a social worker, a psychologist/mental health professional, a medical doctor, an educational guidance counselor, and a member of the Barangay Council for the Protection of Children (BCPC). They work on an individualized intervention plan with the child and the child's family.

To date, there are 19 '*Bahay Pag-asa'* in 18 LGUs in nine regions of the country. Of these, 13 are operational; four have been completed but not yet operational, while two have ceased operations. The children also engage in sports, such as basketball, and spiritual enhancement activities, which include group sharing and bible studies as part of their rehabilitation.

For policy formulation and direction setting, NGOs gave their input in the drafting of the Revised IRR and agency guidelines, and took part in the strategic planning sessions of the Council. As part of their contributions to the attainment of the objectives of the Act, NGOs either established or strengthened their youth homes/facilities or community-based programs. They conducted orientation sessions and awareness campaigns in their partner communities. To date, some published information materials on the Act and other related topics are advocating for the full implementation of the Act.

Local Context of My Study

All children in conflict with the law in Manila are afforded appropriate protection measures as provided for by the United Nations Convention on the Rights of Children (UN CRC) and other relevant international instruments on juvenile justice that promote their dignity and worth as persons, and become active participants of social change.

PNP data shows there had been hundreds of cases involving children aged 11 and under since 2016. But comparing the total for each year, the numbers have considerably and steadily gone down in the past three years.

The Manila Youth Reception Center (MYRC) is a temporary detention center for Juvenile offenders constructed in 1962 as a project of the Juvenile Control Bureau, through the support of the City Mayor, Arsenio H. Lacson, and the Municipal Board of his administration. In the early years of its operation, the center went through the transition of management and supervision from the Manila Police Department to Department of Social Welfare.

Through this mandate, Republic Act 4050 created the Department of Social Welfare on June 18, 1964,. All services, except booking, office investigation and security, were transferred from the Manila Police Department to the Department of Social Welfare. Hence, the center was jointly administered by both agencies from 1964 to 1967.

Finally, in February 1967, the entire management of the center was turned over to the Department of Social Welfare. Since then, police officers from the Manila Police Department have been detailed in the center under the control and supervision of the MYRC chief. Lately, in 1990, with the ratification of the Convention on the Rights of the Child, the management of the center was totally lodged under the Manila Department of Social Welfare, with no police service. The City Government, through the City Security Force, provides security as among the services of the center. Regarding programs, the Division of City Schools has expanded its Special Education for the wards under the *Silahis ng Katarungan* or the other support services; the implementation is in partnership with non-government organizations.

It is also worthwhile to note that several years back, a minor who has violation was called, juvenile delinquent. Under PD 603 "Child and Youth Welfare Code of 1974, they called youthful offenders while in 2006, with the passing into law of RA 9344, Comprehensive Juvenile Justice Welfare Act, a minor with misdemeanor is called, "Child in Conflict the Law" (CICL).

The MYRC is on Arroceros Street (now A. Villegas Street) in Manila, next to the Office of the Ombudsman. It stands on a 990-square-meter lot with the Pasig River at the back and a mini-forest park at the Division of City Schools on the left. The center is a two-storey building with a rectangular open space cutting through its entrance. This space is used as a multi-purpose area for visitors, morning exercises, and laundry-drying area.

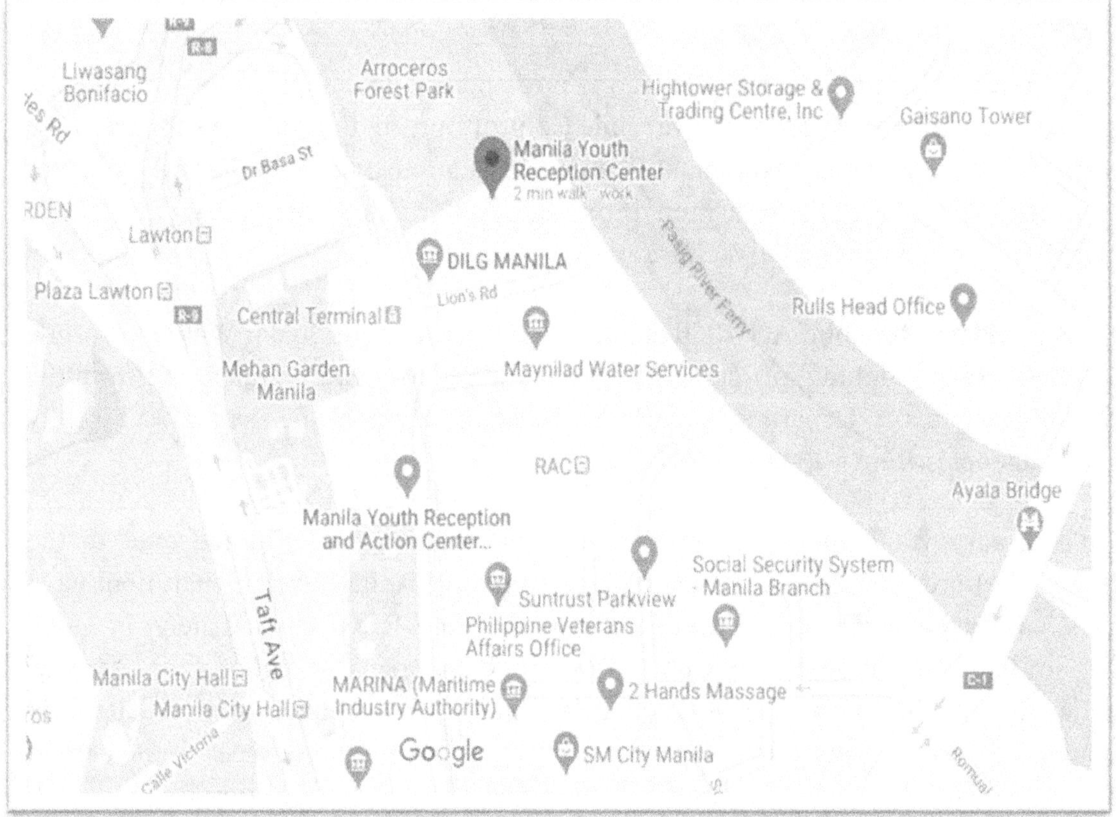

Figure 1. Manila Youth Reception Center Map

It also used as a playground. The entrance to the ground floor is an information table manned by the City Security Force. At this level are the offices of the administrative services and the social services. The mess hall, the kitchen, the medical/dental clinic, the psychosocial intervention room, and the male dormitories are also on the ground floor. The basketball court and the storage rooms are in the backyard. The office of the center chief and the library are on the second floor. The visiting lounge for female residents, the female dormitory, the conference room, the social hall, eight classrooms and the Judges' Lounge are also on the same floor.

The vision of MYRC is to promote the center as an institution where opportunities that recognize and nurture the rights, dignity and potential of children in conflict with the law are available and accessible, and are, thus, instrumental in the attainment of their well-being. Its mission is to provide shelter, utmost care, protection, and guidance to its residents through various programs and services. The MYRC goal is to equip children in conflict with the law adequately with skills, and accordingly prepare them to be responsible citizens once reintegrated back with families and communities. The center's primary objectives are to protect the rights of children in conflict with the law and promote their physical, mental, psychological, and emotional well-being.

The clientele of the center are minors–male and female, 15 years to one day below 18 years old, per R.A. 9344. As of April 2021, 122 (103 male and 19 female) CICLs were under the custody of MYRC. Minors from Manila or non-Manila residents who committed an offense in the City of Manila with imposable penalty on the offense are imprisoned for over 6 years.

Programs and Services of Manila Youth Reception Center

Social Services. The Social Workers conduct admission interviews, social case studies, counseling, group therapy, home visits and sessions with parents of the residents. They also conduct other social activities that allow residents to interact with each other and with selected members of the community. Other services include family counseling and para- legal assistance.

Homelife Services. House parents act as surrogate caregivers; they attend to the basic needs of the residents like food and clothing, referral for medical and dental care, work assignments, and they initiate tutorial activities for slow learner.

Dietary Services. The dietary staff plans and prepares meals for the residents. They also supervise mealtime at the mess hall and maintain the cleanliness and sanitation of the kitchen and other facilities.

Medical Services. The center has an in-house medical officer responsible for the health and physical well-being of residents. Medical services include medical and dental consultation examination, and treatment of ailments of the center residents. They also held lectures on various issues, such as personal hygiene, sanitation and health education. The medical officer, in cooperation with other center personnel, implements a program to cure, detect, prevent and/or control communicable diseases. The medical officer also refers patients to specialist/s or hospitals, and requests for x-ray and laboratory services when needed, and buys medical supplies.

Special Education Program. The DECS, through the DECS-Manila, provides special education services to the residents. Teachers of the Silahis ng Katarungan program use a curriculum emphasizing basic literacy skills, citizenship training, and an integrated vocational program. It is also intended to prepare the residents for the Philippine educational Placement Test.

Administrative Services include coordination with government and non-government agencies regarding such services as procurement of supplies and materials, and general office work, clerical services, janitorial services, maintenance of buildings and facilities.

Security Services includes guard and escort services for residents during court hearings, hospital confinement, educational trips, special home visit, and other activities conducted outside the center.

My Motivation for Doing the Study

My primary motivation to conduct this study is my passion and dedication to provide high quality and effective interventions to people who are in need by inspiring and helping other professionals to be more conscious about the phenomenon of children in conflict with the law. This will be my contribution to the betterment of society and to our fellow service providers.

The number of children-in-conflict with the law, either in institutions or those undergoing diversion/intervention programs in the community, has become increasingly alarming over the years; this has motivated me to conduct this study. As an agent of change helping children of this type, I observe that the number of CICLs has continuously risen; more minors are being admitted to the center. Some of them, after their release from the center, either on bail or through diversion, commit the same offense after barely a month. This made me realize that there are lacking programs and services that need to be delivered for a holistic transformational change.

My passion and commitment to implement more effective and high-quality programs and interventions to address specific needs of children in conflict with the law is brought about by a deeper understanding of children's lives and the entire range of the juvenile justice system. I am motivated to conduct this study because I want to raise the awareness, inspire and advocate for the rights of children in conflict with the law with my colleagues, other professionals and the community through the result of my study.

Statement of the Problem

In this study, I identified CICL who have been reintegrated into their respective family and community after undergoing the rehabilitation program in MYRC. I tried to reflectively analyze their shared lived experiences in their journey towards a second chance to be integrated with their respective family and community. I attempted to get the essence of their lived experiences and drew insight from it. Based on the implications drawn from the study, I explored further recommendations to enrich the programs and services intended for the CICL.

I tried to seek response to the following specific questions:

1. How may the lived experiences of former residents of Manila Youth Reception Center who have been reintegrated with their respective family and community be reflectively described and analyzed?

2. What meanings and insights are derived from their lived experiences?

3. What are the implications of this phenomenological study for social work education and practice and for the field of social work?

Significance of the Study

This study is significant to the following individuals, groups and organizations:

To Government and Non-Government Organizations, this study can serve as a reference to raise their awareness about the significant contribution this can provide to develop CICLs. They may also use this study as the basis for identifying programs for staff development to gain more knowledge in guiding their clients to their journey to transformation.

To service providers who are professionals that accompany the CICLs on their transformational journey to be reintegrated into their respective family and community, they may refer to this study to assess how they deliver or provide their service to their CICL clients. This study may serve as reference to come up with creative and transformative ideas that will allow them to develop effective and efficient approach to deal with CICLs and create a good citizen in them.

To social work professionals, I hope this study may awaken their consciousness about the collective lived experiences of CICLs. This study hopes to help them validate their own experiences and be able to check their level of consciousness regarding their own journey in working with CICLs. Also, this study may be referred in re-assessing themselves towards developing and enhancing the delivery of service to CICL.

To the community, this study will make people in the community aware about the unique challenges and difficulties experienced by CICL to change for the better. This study intends to make the community understand the context of CICL dilemmas in the provision and delivery of effective programs and services. This study also allows the community to see the perspectives of service providers; thus, enhance their understanding of a compassionate service delivery.

To the CICL, this study hopes to make them understand their world through their lived experiences; and to realize the different situations and dilemmas they encounter may lead them to an enhanced understanding of their perspective and their journey towards transformation.

To families and families of CICL, in particular, this study intends to make them aware of the unique challenges and difficulties experienced by CICLs in their journey to change or transform. This study also aims to make families better understand the dilemma faced by CICLs in terms of provision and delivery of effective programs and services. May this study allow families to see the viewpoints of service providers and may they realize the relevance of compassionate family rearing patterns in order for children to avoid being in conflict with the law.

To the school, which task is to train and form children and adults with the right attitude, good manners and right conduct, thus shape the personality of a child, this study will to make schools realize the role they play in developing a child to become a better citizen. May this study make schools cognizant of their role and be able to apply new ways or approaches to transform and develop the full potential of students.

With children who are already in conflict with the law, may this study inspire them to develop new ways and method to be integrated into their curriculum, vision, mission, and goals.

To professors, this study may enhance academic teaching method and their perspectives enriched by integrating and developing curriculum that focuses on the delivery of effective interventions to CICL. Professors may refer to this study to enhance their teaching methods and perspectives in the social work profession. Professors may also use this study as a reference to develop and training new social work students on dealing with effective delivery of service to their profession.

To social worker students, this study may be used as reference to enlighten and awaken them towards an understanding of the importance of effective interventions in terms of service delivery to CICLs that is transformative, and to prepare them for challenges and difficulties in their future work as professional social workers.

To churches, this study can raise the consciousness of church people about the plight of CICL and the need for ministers who could develop CICL's spirituality with compassion. The church could integrate in their programs and services a more effective spiritual service to CICLs.

To policy makers, this study can be used as a reference to review ethical professional standards and develop an effective intervention and delivery of service for CICLs. This study hopes to enlighten policy-makers about the difficulties experienced by CICL, thus, find better way to resolve the issue by implementing new policies that integrate spirituality and compassionate care.

To the Asian Social Institute, this study hopes to contribute to a breakthrough in coming up with transformative strategies to develop CICLs into becoming good citizens. A deeper analysis of the issue based on the lived experiences and series of reflections, programs and services may be developed and proposed as part of the curriculum of social work profession.

Scope and Limitations of the Study

I focus my study on six male CICL co-researchers aged 16-18 years. The CICLs have been reintegrated with their family and community for one year. Currently, they are immersed/reintegrated into their community. I selected them from the different areas in NCR. They used to be clients of Manila Youth Rehabilitation Center (MYRC) and have availed of the different programs and services provided to Children in Conflict with the Law. MYRC is in the National Capital Region where more CICLs abound.

With phenomenology as the method I use in this study, I gathered the lived experiences of my co-researchers through an in-depth interview guide by some interview questions specifically constructed to have a deeper understanding of the lives of my co-researchers. The in-depth interview yielded a self-narrative report with art symbols. Gathering of lived experiences/narratives and other social facts took 8 months, June 2020 to February 2021.

Definition of Terms

Child or Children refers/refer to persons below eighteen years of age or those over but cannot take care of themselves fully or protect themselves from abuse, neglect, cruelty, exploitation or discrimination because of physical or mental disability or condition. (IRR, R.A. 7610). In this study, it refers to person/s living in Manila, incapable of taking care of and protecting themselves and vulnerable to make offence with the law.

'Children in Conflict with the Law' (CICL) refers to anyone under 18 who comes into contact with the justice system because of being suspected or accused of committing an offence (UNICEF). In this study, it refers to children who are suspected or accused of committing an offence in Manila, Philippines.

Center, in this study, refers to the Manila Youth Reception Center (MYRC), a temporary detention center for children in conflict with the law who commit an offence in Manila.

Conflict is an active disagreement between opposing opinions or needs, according to Cambridge dictionary. In this study, it refers to the offence committed by a child against the law as mandated by the Philippines.

Delinquency is a criminal behavior carried out by a juvenile. Depending on the nation of origin, a juvenile becomes an adult anywhere between the ages of 15 to 18, although the age is sometimes lowered for murder and other serious crimes. Delinquency implies conduct that does not conform to the legal or moral standards of society; it usually applies only to acts that, if performed by an adult, would be termed criminal. It is thus distinguished from a status offense, a term applied in the United States and other national legal systems, to acts considered wrongful when committed by a juvenile but not when committed by an adult (Britannica Encyclopaedia). In this study, it refers to showing or characterized by a tendency to commit crime, particularly minor crime.

Interview is a face-to-face meeting usually between two people. In social work, it is used to gather or give information, give therapy, resolve a disagreement, or consider a joint undertaking (De Guzman, 1998). This is the tool being used by the social worker to gather social facts from the children. It is a one-on-one conversation between the child and the social worker.

Journey is an act or instance of traveling from one place to another, something suggesting travel or passage from one place to another, according to Merriam-Webster dictionary. In this study, journey means what motivates us, what drives us, and what engages us. It is what makes life worth ling, what makes each of us unique, what brings us joy and suffering that allows us to learn something. This is the path taken by children in conflict with the law to fulfill their purpose of existence in the universe.

Social Work is a practice-based profession and an academic discipline that promotes social change and development, social cohesion, and the empowerment and liberation of people. Principles of social justice, human rights, collective responsibility and respect for diversities are central to social work. Underpinned by theories of social work, social sciences, humanities and indigenous knowledge, social work engages people and structures to address life challenges and enhance wellbeing. (IFSW, 2014). In this study, it refers to the licensed profession concerned with helping children in conflict with the law to enhance their individual and collective well-being. It aims to help people develop their skills and their ability to use their own resources and those of the community to resolve problems.

Transformative means causing a major change to something or someone, especially in a way that makes it or him/her better, according to the Cambridge dictionary. In this study, it means a transformative learning from the lived experiences of my co-researchers that cause a shift in an individual's perspective. It is because learning is making a new or revised interpretation of the meaning of an experience. It is a path of enlightenment from their journey as children in conflict with the law.

Chapter II

THEORETICAL ORIENTATION, REVIEW OF RELATED LITERATURE AND STUDIES

In this chapter, I present the fundamental theories that I used as a frame of reference for my study, along with the related literature and studies I gathered, which I believe best explain the subject I am studying. These likewise provide a clearer picture of the phenomenon I wish to understand.

Theoretical Orientation

A. Psychosocial Stages of Erik Erikson

Erik Erikson (1950, 1963) does not talk about psychosexual stages. He discusses psychosocial stages. Freud influenced his ideas, going along with Freud's (1923) theory regarding the structure and topography of personality.

However, whereas Freud was an id psychologist, Erikson was an ego psychologist. He emphasized the role of culture and society and the conflicts that can take place within the ego itself, whereas Freud emphasized the conflict between the id and the superego. According to Erikson, the ego develops as it successfully resolves crises that are distinctly social in nature. These involve establishing a sense of trust in others, developing a sense of identity in society, and helping the next generation prepare for the future.

Erikson extends on Freudian thoughts by focusing on the adaptive and creative characteristic of the ego, and expanding the notion of the stages of personality development to include the entire lifespan.

Erikson proposed a lifespan model of development, taking in five stages up to the age of 18 years and three further stages beyond, well into adulthood. He suggests that there is still plenty of room for continued growth and development throughout one's life. Erikson puts a great deal of emphasis on the adolescent period, feeling it was a crucial stage for developing a person's identity.

Like Freud and many others, Erik Erikson maintained that personality develops in a predetermined order, and builds upon each previous stage. I call this the epigenetic principle. The outcome of this 'maturation timetable' is a wide and integrated set of life skills and abilities that function together within the autonomous individual. However, instead of focusing on sexual development (like Freud), he was interested in how children socialize and how this affects their sense of self.

Erikson's (1959) theory of psychosocial development has eight distinct stages. Like Freud, Erikson assumes that a crisis occurs at each stage of development. For Erikson (1963), these crises are psychosocial because they involve psychological needs of the individual (i.e. psycho) conflicting with the needs of society (i.e. social).

According to the theory, successful completion of each stage results in a healthy personality and the acquisition of basic virtues. Basic virtues are characteristic strengths which the ego can use to resolve subsequent crises. Failure to complete successfully, a stage can cause a reduced ability to complete further stages and therefore unhealthier personality and sense of self. These stages, however, can be resolved successfully later.

Table 1. Psychosocial Stages
(http://www.simplypsychology.org/Erik-Erikson.html)

Stage	Psychosocial Crisis	Basic Virtue	Age
1	Trust vs. mistrust	Hope	Infancy (o to1 ½)
2	Autonomy vs. shame	Will	Early Childhood (1 ½ to3)
3	Initiative vs. guilt	Purpose	Play Age (3 to 5)
4	Industry vs. inferiority	Competency	School Age (5 to 12)
5	Ego identity vs. Role Confusion	Fidelity	Adolescence (12 to 18)
6	Intimacy vs. isolation	Love	Young Adult (18 to 40)
7	Generativity vs. stagnation	Care	Adult hood(40 to 65)
8	Ego integrity vs. despair	Wisdom	Maturity (65+)

Classical Conditioning

Ivan Pavlov was a Russian psychologist best known for his work in classical conditioning. In 1904, this work earned him the Nobel Prize in physiology or medicine. His principles have been applied to behavior therapies in educational classrooms and to reduce phobias via systematic desensitization.

Pavlovian theory is a learning procedure that involves pairing a stimulus with a conditioned response. In the famous experiments that Ivan Pavlov conducted with his dogs, Pavlov found that objects or events could trigger a conditioned response. The experiments began with Pavlov showing how the presence of a bowl of dog food (stimulus) would trigger an unconditioned response (salivation). But Pavlov noticed the dogs associated his lab assistant with food, creating a learned and conditioned response. This was an important scientific discovery.

Pavlov then designed an experiment using a bell as a neutral stimulus. As he gave food to the dogs, he rang the bell. Then, after repeating this procedure, he tried ringing the bell without providing food to the dogs. On its own, an increase in salivation occurred. The result of the experiment was a new conditioned response in the dogs.

Pavlov's theory later developed into classical conditioning, which refers to learning that associates an unconditioned stimulus that already results in a response (such as a reflex) with a new conditioned stimulus. As a result, the new stimulus brings about the same response.

Operant conditioning stories involve an animal doing something that changes the world in a way that produces, crudely, a good or a bad outcome. When an organism does something that is followed by a good outcome, that behavior will become more likely in the future. When an organism does something that is followed by a bad outcome, that behavior will become less likely in the future.

The action and outcome could coincide because of natural laws or social conventions, because someone purposely set it up that way, or maybe the events followed because of random chance in this animal's life history.

Operant Conditioning of B.F. Skinner

B. F. Skinner was one of the most influential of American psychologists. A behaviorist, he developed the theory of operant conditioning — the idea that behavior is determined by its consequences, be they reinforcements or punishments, which make it more or less likely that the behavior will occur again. Skinner believed that the only scientific approach to psychology was one that studied behaviors, not internal (subjective) mental processes.

B. F. Skinner's theory is based on operant conditioning. The organism is in the process of "operating" on the environment, which in ordinary terms means it is bouncing around its world, doing what it does. During this "operating," the organism encounters a special stimulus, called a reinforcing stimulus, or simply a reinforcer. This special stimulus has the effect of increasing the operant - the behavior occurring just before the reinforcer. This is operant conditioning: "a consequence follows the behavior, and the nature of the consequence changes the organism's tendency to repeat the behavior in the future."

Skinner conducted research on shaping behavior through positive and negative reinforcement and showed operant conditioning, a behavior modification technique which he developed in contrast with classical conditioning. His idea of the behavior modification technique was to put the subject on a program with steps. The steps would set goals which would help you determine how the subject would be changed by following the steps. The program design helps the subject reach the desired state. Then, the implementation and evaluation put the program to use and then evaluate its effectiveness.

Skinner did not advocate the use of punishment. His primary focus was to target behavior and see that consequences deliver responses. From his research came "shaping" (described above) which is described as creating behaviors through reinforcing. He also came up with the example of a child's refusal to go to school and that the focus should be on what is causing the child's refusal, not necessarily the refusal itself. His research suggested that punishment was an ineffective way of controlling behavior, leading to short-term behavior change, but resulting mostly in the subject attempting to avoid the punishing stimulus instead of avoiding the behavior that was causing punishment. A simple example of this, he believed, was the failure of prison to eliminate criminal behavior. If prison (as a punishing stimulus) was effective at altering behavior, there would be no criminality, since the risk of imprisonment for criminal conduct is well established, Skinner deduced. However, he noted that individuals still commit offences, but attempt to avoid discovery and therefore punishment. He noted that the punishing stimulus does not stop criminal behavior; the criminal simply becomes more sophisticated at avoiding the punishment. Reinforcement, both positive and negative (the latter of which is often confused with punishment), he believed, proved to be more effective in bringing about lasting changes in behavior.

Behavior modification — often referred to as b-mod — is the therapy technique based on Skinner's work. It is very straight-forward: Extinguish an undesirable behavior (by removing the reinforcer) and replace it with a desirable behavior by reinforcement. It has been used on many psychological problems — addictions, neuroses, shyness, autism, even schizophrenia — and works particularly well with children. There are examples of back-ward psychotics who haven't communicated with others for years who have been conditioned to behave themselves in fairly normal ways, such as eating with a knife and fork, taking care of their own hygiene needs, dressing themselves, and so on.

There is an offshoot of b-mod called the token economy. This is primarily used in institutions such as psychiatric hospitals, juvenile halls, and prisons. Certain rules are made explicit in the institution, and behaving yourself appropriately is rewarded with tokens — poker chips, tickets, funny money, recorded notes, etc. Certain poor behavior is also often followed by a withdrawal of these tokens. The tokens can be traded in for desirable things such as candy, cigarettes, games, movies, time out of the institution, and so on. This has been very effective in maintaining order in these often difficult institutions. stages, however, can be resolved successfully later.

Social Learning Theory (Albert Bandura)

The social learning theory of Bandura emphasizes the importance of observing and modeling the behaviors, attitudes, and emotional reactions of others. Bandura (1977) states: "Learning would be exceedingly laborious, not to mention hazardous, if people had to rely solely on the effects of their own actions to inform them of what to do. Fortunately, most human behavior is learned observationally through modeling: from observing others one forms an idea of how new behaviors are performed, and on later occasions this coded information serves as a guide for action." Social learning theory explains human behavior in terms of continuous reciprocal interaction between cognitive, behavioral, environmental influences.

The component processes underlying observational learning is: (1) Attention, including modeled events (distinctiveness, affective valence, complexity, prevalence, functional value) and observer characteristics (sensory capacities, arousal level, perceptual set, past reinforcement), (2) Retention, including symbolic coding, cognitive organization, symbolic rehearsal, motor rehearsal), (3) Motor Reproduction, including physical capabilities, self-observation of reproduction, accuracy of feedback, and (4) Motivation, including external, vicarious and self reinforcement.

Because it encompasses attention, memory and motivation, social learning theory spans both cognitive and behavioral frameworks. Bandura's theory improves upon the strictly behavioral interpretation of modeling provided by Miller & Dollard (1941). Bandura's work is related to the theories of Vygotsky and Lave, which also emphasize the central role of social learning.

Social learning theory has been applied extensively to the understanding of aggression (Bandura, 1973) and psychological disorders, particularly in behavior modification (Bandura, 1969). It is also the theoretical foundation for the technique of behavior modeling, which is widely used in training programs. In recent years, Bandura has focused his work on the concept of self-efficacy in a variety of contexts (e.g., Bandura, 1997).

According to social learning theory, juveniles learn to engage in crime in the same way they learn to engage in conforming behavior: through association with or exposure to others. In fact, association with delinquent friends is the best predictor of delinquency other than prior delinquency.

The Modeling Process developed by Bandura helps us understand that not all observed behaviors could be learned effectively, nor learning can cause behavioral changes.

Social learning theory suggests that human behavior is learned as individuals interact with their environment. Problem behavior is maintained by positive or negative reinforcement. Cognitive- behavioral therapy looks at what role thoughts play in maintaining the problem. Emphasis is on changing dysfunctional thoughts which influence behavior. It is also methods which stem from this theory that influence the gradual shaping of new behavior through positive and negative reinforcement, modeling, stress management: biofeedback, relaxation techniques, cognitive restructuring, imagery and systematic desensitization.

Family System Theory (Murray Bowen)

Family systems theory is a concept of looking at the family as a cohesive emotional unit. According to this theory, family members are intensely emotionally connected. Psychiatrist Murray Bowen developed the family systems theory. Regarding the family systems theory, Dr. Bowen was described as "one of those rare human beings who had a genuinely new idea."

The family systems theory states that a family functions as a system wherein each member plays a specific role and must follow certain rules. Based on the roles within the system, people are expected to interact with and respond to one another in a certain way. Patterns develop within the system, and each member's behaviors impact the other members in predictable ways. Depending on the specific system, these behavioral patterns can lead to either balance or dysfunction of the system- or both, at various points in time.

According to Dr. Bowen's theory, even when people may feel they are disconnected from members of their family, the family still has a profound impact on their emotions and actions-whether positive or negative. And, a change in one person sparks a change in how other members of the family unit act and feel as well. Though interdependence can vary between different families, all families have some level of it among the members.

Dr. Bowen believes perhaps humans developed to be interdependent on family members to promote cooperation among families that are necessary for things like shelter and protection. But, in stressful situations, the anxiety that one person feels can spread among family members and the interdependence becomes emotionally taxing rather than comforting.

There will always be one person in the family unit who "absorbs" the bulk of the emotions of other members of the family, and this person is most likely to suffer from things like depression, alcoholism, and physical illness. This shows the importance of families working together to conquer their problems, rather than letting negative emotions stew. Therapy or counseling can help many families work better together and keep anxieties at a minimum.

Family relationships of CICL are very complex, and no two families are exactly alike. Despite these differences, some theories suggest all families fall into the same model of the emotional system. This concept is referred to as the Family Systems Theory.

Moral Development Theory of Lawrence Kolhberg

The numbers of children in conflict with the law continue to rise, yet few studies have been conducted regarding factors associated with it. It has been theorized that children with conduct disorder represent most children in conflict with the law, and that poor moral competence mediates the association between conduct disorder and antisocial behavior.

Kohlberg's theory proposes that there are three levels of moral development, with each level split into two stages. Kohlberg suggested people move through these stages in a fixed order, and that moral understanding is linked to cognitive development. The three levels of moral reasoning include pre-conventional, conventional, and post-conventional.

By using children's responses to a series of moral dilemmas, Kohlberg established that the reasoning behind the decision was a greater sign of moral development than the actual answer. Lawrence Kohlberg (1958) agreed with Piaget's (1932) theory of moral development in principle but wanted to develop his ideas further.

He used Piaget's storytelling technique to tell people stories involving moral dilemmas. In each case, he presented a choice to be considered, for example, between the rights of some authority and the needs of some deserving individual who is being unfairly treated.

Moral Development theory of Lawrence Kohlberg was the basis of the DSWD's instrument on assessment of discernment. It may relate to an assessment of whether the rehabilitation program enhanced the CICL's level of discernment, the capability to control impulses are sustained and the challenges of re-offending are managed adequately.

Strengths-based approaches for working with individuals

Strengths-based practice is a collaborative process between the person supported by services and those supporting them, allowing them to work together to determine an outcome that draws on the person's strengths and assets. It concerns itself principally with the quality of the relationship that develops between those providing and being supported, as well as the elements that the person seeking support brings to the process (Duncan and Hubble, 2000). Working collaboratively promotes the opportunity for individuals to be co-producers of services and support rather than solely consumers of those services (Morgan and Ziglio, 2007).

With the growing focus on self-directed support (Scottish Government, 2010a), self-management of illness and long-term conditions (Scottish Government, 2008a), and working together to achieve better outcomes (Christie, 2011), there is increasing interest in identifying and building on the strengths and capacities of those supported by services, to help them resolve problems and deliver their own solutions. Strengths-based approaches concentrate on the inherent strengths of individuals, families, groups and organisations, deploying personal strengths to aid recovery and empowerment. To focus on health and well-being is to embrace an asset-based approach where the goal is to promote the positive.

Many are of the view that use of strengths-based approaches will be instrumental in successfully shifting the balance of care, and develop services that are focused on prevention and independence (Scottish Government, 2010b). This will challenge social services' historical focus on clients' deficiencies to a focus on possibilities and solutions (Saleebey, 2006). In effect, the strengths' perspective is the social work equivalent in emphasizing the origins of strength and resilience. It argues against the dominance of a problem-focused perspective.

Some researchers have criticized strengths-based approaches citing that they are not in fact new from many other traditional approaches (McMillen, Morris and Sherraden, 2004) and that they are not based on evidence of efficacy (Staudt, Howard and Drake, 2001). Indeed, as interest has grown in this perspective, members of different disciplines in the sector are trying more positive approaches and using different words to describe it. Prevention practitioners use words such as 'resilience' to describe an individual's ability to function well and achieve goals despite overbearing stresses or challenges, like the children in conflict with the law reintegrated to their communities.

Rapp, Saleebey and Sullivan (2008) offer six standards for judging what makes up a strengths-based approach. Practitioners may like to use the following list to consider their own practice. The standards include:

Goal orientation: Strengths-based practice is goal oriented. The central and most crucial element of any approach is the extent to which people themselves set goals they would like to achieve in their lives.

Strengths assessment: The primary focus is not on problems or deficits, and the individual is supported to recognize the inherent resources they have at their disposal which they can use to counteract any difficulty or condition.

Resources from the environment: Strength's proponents believe that in every environment there are individuals, associations, groups and institutions who have something to give, that others may find useful, and that it may be the practitioner's role to enable links to these resources.

Explicit methods are used for identifying client and environmental strengths for goal attainment: These methods will be different for each of the strengths-based approaches. For example, in solution-focused therapy, clients will be helped set goals before the identification of strengths, whilst in strengths-based case management; individuals will go through a specific 'strengths assessment.

The relationship is hope-inducing: A strengths-based approach aims to increase the hopefulness of the client. Further, hope can be realized through strengthened relationships with people, communities, and culture.

Meaningful choice: Strengths proponents highlight a collaborative stance where people are experts in their own lives and the practitioner's role is to increase and explain choices and encourage people to make their own decisions and informed choices.

Strengths-based approaches can work on several levels - from individuals, associations and organizations right through to communities (Foot and Hopkins, 2010). There are rapidly burgeoning methods of practice being developed that are related to, and build upon, the fundamental building blocks of the strengths' perspective. Some of these methods can and will be used alongside others, and some may be used in isolation. The focus of this insight is to better understand the use of a strengths perspective for transforming relationships between practitioners and people who are supported by services.

Empirical research suggests that strengths-based interventions have a positive psychological impact, particularly in enhancing individual well-being through development of hope. In a pilot study of people with serious mental health issues, people were asked to identify the factors that they saw as critical to recovery. The most important elements identified included the ability to have hope, as well as developing trust in one's own thoughts and judgments (Ralph, Lambric and Steele, 1996). The aim of strengths-based practice is to enable people to look beyond their immediate and real problems and dare to conceive a future that inspires them, providing hope that things can improve. Strength-based approaches are effective in developing and maintaining hope in individuals, and consequently many studies cite evidence for enhanced well-being (Smock, Weltchler, McCollum et al, 2008). Through having high expectations for individuals, strengths-based practitioners create a climate of optimism, hope, and possibility, which has been shown to have successful outcomes, particularly in work with families (Hopps, Pinderhughes, and Shankar, 1995).

Review of Related Literature

A. Foreign Literature

Punishing Children: A survey of criminal responsibility and approaches across Europe: This survey of youth justice systems in Europe emphasizes the extent to which England and Wales is divorced from our neighbors in the way we see children and the way we treat them when they do something wrong. Most European countries see a child committing crime as a welfare matter, an occasion to energize the various child welfare agencies to examine what is causing the child's offending behaviour and to address those causes–be it educational difficulties, mental health needs or histories of abuse and neglect. By comparison, we engineered our system to respond primarily through punishment. Given the continuing degree to which 'youth crime' is an issue of great public concern–for example, knife crime among inner city teenage boys–it is unclear what decades of a punitive system has achieved in making both children who offend and the public at large safe from crime.

Not that the welfare of children in our youth justice system is ignored entirely. The trend over the last 10 years and the justice reforms of the current government have seen an increasing blurring of the lines between what should properly be social welfare policy and what is criminal justice policy. In the government's most recent publication, the Youth Crime Action Plan (Home Office et al. 2008), this trend continues to cause concern. Rather than empowering local authorities children's services to address the needs of the whole child and not simply the child as offender, the government continues to plough the expensive but failed furrow of delivering social welfare to children via ever multiplying criminal justice agencies. With the promotion in the Youth Crime Action Plan of such policy ideas as non-negotiable support, the government threatens to widen the net for criminal justice responses even further–with children and their families at ever-increasing threat of sanction in order to comply.

Many juvenile justice systems are rooted in a preventative and rehabilitative ethos while attempting at the same time to satisfy perceived public anxieties with harsher custodial sentences for serious crimes or even persistent minor offending. The extremely low age of criminal responsibility in England and Wales, despite the overall preventative purpose of the youth justice system, is an acute example of this.

The overall result is an increase in the number of children passing through criminal justice systems, although most jurisdictions report that youth crime figures have decreased or are stable.

Teens Who Commit Crimes: According to this article, Children are not born with a built-in set of the rules of morality, nor do they suddenly wake up one day as criminals. Lessons in ethics and manners have to start at home. They need to be reminded about it and reinforced by the examples parents set as to the consequences should those rules not be followed. These guidelines are fostered throughout the child's life — at schools, among friends and during religious and extra-curricular activities.

But with moral lines so blurred in today's culture, children need extra help to distinguish between rules that are condoned in violent video games, rap music and films that glorify criminal behavior from those that apply to real life. Bottom line: It's the family's responsibility to watch for signals when those lines are dangerously crossed and to decide if authorities should be notified when real life rules are disobeyed. It's a decision that depends not only on the age of the child and the severity and chronicity of their crime, but on parental attitudes as well.

Clearly, for a child being a danger to themselves or others, there is no debate — the behavior has to be reported to authorities. But for all the in-between offenses, this is where families must play an active role early on creating clear guidelines for both children and parent. Unacceptable behavior needs to be clarified. Consequences need to be unambiguous. Follow-through must occur in a loving and caring atmosphere.

Clarity about lesser "crimes" helps kids avoid committing more serious ones. By the time a teen is capable of murder, parents must turn them in, of course. But, perhaps if children are raised dealing with the more gentle "authorities at home," these kinds of tragedies would be avoided.

B. Local Literature

Holistic Development Program for Children in Conflict with the Law at Social Development Center, Bacolod City, Negros Occidental Philippines: Social Development Center (SDC), Bacolod City, Negros Occidental Philippines entitled the Holistic Development Program for Children in conflict with the law to empower and rehabilitate the children through transformational activities, projects and programs through a holistic and creative approach.

The SDC is a rehabilitation center for children who come into contact with the justice system because of being suspected or accused of committing an offence. These children are commonly known as Children in Conflict with the Law (CICL). The Social Development Center served as a transformational facility only for youth offenders of Bacolod City, Negros Occidental. SDC is also focused on rehabilitating and empowering CICL while they are housed in, so that they will become productive members of society. However, unaddressed problems that negatively affect the system and rehabilitation of SDC were observed. These include unsanitary installations, lack of basic needs including emotional and mental needs, and lack of interventions for empowerment, growth and rehabilitation of CICL. Because of the existing problems, these hinder the empowerment and rehabilitation of CICL, which eventually leads to degradation of society where criminal rates would increase, where drugs are rampant, and where violence would continue to persist over peace.

This motivated the proponent to give interventions to CICL by conducting creative transformational activities, projects, and programs at the Social Development Center for the holistic development of the CICL. The holistic development program was focused and benefited Children in Conflict with the Law (CICL) in Social Development Center, Bacolod City. The Children in Conflict with the Law, housed in SDC, are children in Bacolod City under 18 who come into contact with the justice system because of being suspected or accused of committing an offence.

In solution to the existing problems, the proponent, in partnership with other non-government organizations, school-based organizations and private foundations, has conducted activities in the SDC focused on different categories namely, intellectual, psychological, spiritual, skills training, arts and culture, and environmental.

One activity under the program is the Boy Scouts Auxiliary Brigade. This activity aims to use the ideals, values and principles of scouting as an instrument in indoctrinating these wayward youths with the virtues of love of God, country, and fellowmen towards molding them into responsible and conscientious citizens, and to transform them, from being criminal elements, into crime watchers and peacemakers when they go back to their respective communities.

The Boy Scouts Auxiliary Brigade was a conducted to give the CICL a series of scouting training for them to become productive members of the society when they go out from SDC. Forty (40) youth offenders took part in the activities and 35 of them were donned with scout neckerchief during the investiture ceremony as a sign of the culmination of their hard work for the 7-day program.

Lawmaker admits PH has no facilities for child offenders (Sunstar): The Chair of the House committee on justice Salvador "Doy" Leachon admitted that the country is not yet ready for the enactment of the bill lowering the age of criminal liability from 15 years old to nine years old.

During the period of sponsorship and debate on House Bill No. 8858 or "An Act Expanding the Juvenile Justice and Welfare System and Strengthening the Social Reintegration Programs for Children in Conflict with the Law, Amending for the Purpose Republic Act No. 9344, as amended, otherwise known as the 'Juvenile Justice and Welfare Act of 2006, Bukidnon Rep. Miguel Zubiri asked Leachon if the government is ready to attend to the needs of every child in conflict with the law.

The debate on the bill happened on Tuesday, January 22, just a day after the committee on justice approved House Bill 8858. Because of the lack of infrastructure or facilities by the agencies involved, our children will end up in the slammer or jail, whether temporarily or permanently.

According to Zubiri, there is no space for jails in DSWD and some areas are not developed. He also noted that while other countries, including Japan have a minimum age of criminal liability that is lower than what is proposed in the Congress, he noted that these countries, Japan specifically, are more developed than the Philippines and can provide the facilities needed for the children offenders.

Zubiri appealed to the members of the House as he ended his manifestation: "Be very careful in deciding especially for the future of our children because they are watching us and they know we are here for them to protect their rights at all cost."

Under the bill, children aged nine and above at the time of the commission of the offense would be exempted from criminal liability and be subjected to an intervention program unless the child has acted with discernment.

Silencing opposing views, Leachon earlier said the bill is "pro-children" and that the children in conflict with the law will not be jailed nor will they be mixed with prisoners but will only be confined in *Bahay Pag-asa*, a transformational facility only for the children in conflict with the law.

The bill mandates the creation of *Bahay Pag-asa* in strategic locations in provinces and imposes mandatory counseling for parents. It also mandates the DSWD to operate *Bahay Pag-asa*. The funding for the facility shall be included in the budget for the DSWD in the General Appropriations Act, as stated under the bill.

Not to fail our children by: Anna Marie V. Alhambra–inquirerdotnet: A decade after the Juvenile Justice and Welfare Act (JJWA) was enacted, it now faces its biggest challenge. Among the priority bills of President Duterte and his allies in Congress is the lowering of the minimum age of criminal responsibility (MACR) from 15 to 9 years old.

The MACR is the lowest age by which a person can be charged in court and be jailed. Several bills filed in the House of Representatives to lower the MACR argue children are "getting bolder and braver" and are being used by syndicates in committing crimes. This reasoning overlooks the fact that in the JJWA, children in conflict with the law (CICL) do not go scot-free, but are held responsible according to their age and developmental capacities. Children below 15 years who commit crimes are not charged in court, but they must undergo intervention programs and are required to pay damages to their victims. The JJWA provides a separate justice system for children, acknowledging their different physical, social, and psychological capacities from those of adults.

If our government is serious about stopping children from committing crimes, it must pursue the full implementation of the JJWA instead of lowering the MACR. Full implementation of the JJWA requires having prevention, intervention, diversion, and rehabilitation programs and child-friendly institutions. This further requires the commitment of competent duty-bearers and sufficient funds for implementing the law.

The 2014 independent evaluation of *Bahay Pag-asa* (BPAs) and regional rehabilitation centers for youth (RRCYs) by UNICEF identified factors that negatively and significantly affect the rehabilitation and reintegration of CICL. Two of these are the insufficient capacity of juvenile justice actors (i.e., social workers, police, etc.), and the weak commitment of local government units (LGUs) in implementing programs for CICL.

The insufficient capacity of juvenile justice actors is because of a lack of knowledge of programs that can be done in the areas of prevention, intervention, and diversion. This leads to "erroneous or limited application of the programs." Among LGUs, it was observed that the lack of training "leads to misunderstandings, even resistance" by implementers. In our training sessions with the Barangay Councils for the Protection of Children, members admitted to lacking not just knowledge of the law but also skills in handling CICL cases. Intervention—a program to address issues that cause the child to commit an offense—is often neglected. Intervention is an individualized treatment program that may include counseling, education and skills training, medical attention, and participation in community or school activities.

The weak commitment of LGUs in implementing programs for CICL is also because of limited financial resources. The 2014 evaluation by UNICEF elaborated that limited financial resources are clear in the lack of BPAs in most regions. The law mandates provinces and highly urbanized cities to have BPAs—24-hour child-caring institutions for CICL above 15 and below 18 awaiting court disposition and CICL above 12 and below 15 who committed serious and repeat offenses. Information from the Juvenile Justice and Welfare Council shows that out of 114 expected BPAs, only 35 are operational. BPAs perform more poorly compared to RRCYs in providing the basic needs of children because the latter receive stable funding from the national government. This is also clear in the 2016 study by the Philippine Legislators' Committee on Population and Development and UNICEF, where results show that LGUs with minimal financial resources and personnel with low individual capacities are likely to have little awareness of child protection laws, including JJWA.

Instead of lowering the MACR, legislators should strengthen the full implementation of JJWA to prevent children from offending and re-offending. Children should not suffer because of what our institutions have failed to do.

The University of St. La Salle - *Bahay Pag-asa* Youth Center: The *BAHAY PAG-ASA* YOUTH CENTER operates as a transformational facility only for Children-in-Conflict with the Law (CICL) and Children-at-Risk (CAR) from Negros Occidental and surrounding areas. Through the center, they aim to administer a holistic formation/transformational program with emphasis on basic education, spiritual formation, life skills and livelihood skills; Provide competent and committed legal services which will include non-formal learning modules on criminal behavior and its consequences; Provide an interfaced support system for the youth offenders after their release composed of the family, the school or workplace, the church, and the community to ensure successful re-integration; and pilot, assess and improve the program so that it may serve as a model for youth rehabilitation, which may be replicated in other areas of the country.

The University of St. La Salle (USLS), inspired by the work of its Founder, St. John Baptiste de la Salle, commits to respond to the growing needs of a special group of children and youth, the Children-In-Contact with the Law (CICL), in the Provinces of Negros Occidental and Guimaras, through the establishment the USLS - Bahay Pag-asa Youth Center (USLS-BPYC).

In collaboration and partnership with the Department of Social Welfare and Development (DSWD), Department of Justice (DOJ), Bureau of Jail Management and Penology (BJMP), the Local Government Units (LGUs), the Provincial Government and other government organization (GO), non-government organizations (NGOs), volunteer individuals and groups, the USLS-*Bahay Pag-asa* Youth Center (USLS-BPYC) aimed to promote quality education through intervention, diversion and rehabilitation programs and services that seeks to address the best interest, welfare and development of the children and youth at risks, forming them into becoming a self-reliant, productive and God-fearing individuals, upon reintegration with their families and in the community.

Inspired by the Charism of the Founder, St. John Baptiste de la Salle, and animated by Christian values, the University seeks to help our people, especially the poor, live a life of dignity to the fullest of their capabilities. As a catalyst for change, it commits itself to install concern for the environment, community, and country. All these, in the Lasallian spirit of faith and zeal: to do everything for God and to attribute all to God.

The University of St. La Salle is a Catholic institution committed to the holistic formation of the youth. It promotes quality of education responsive to the global realities and to the call of the Church for evangelization. It aims to foster a culture of openness and dialogue in all sectors of the Lasallian Family. Inspired by the Charism of the Founder, St. John Baptiste de la Salle, and animated by Christian values, the University seeks to help our people, especially the poor, live a life of dignity to the fullest of their capabilities. As a catalyst for change, it commits itself to install concern for the environment, community, and country.

_Review of Related Studies

A. Foreign Studies

What our new study on juvenile justice in ASEAN countries reveals (Fair and Efficient Justice 14 April 2015): Christian Ranheim, Head of RWI's Jakarta office, presents a study on juvenile justice in the ASEAN region at the 13th UN Congress on Crime Prevention and Criminal Justice in Doha, Qatar The Raoul Wallenberg Institute reported today that concludes that the number of juveniles below the age of 18 who are deprived of their liberty in ASEAN (Association of Southeast Asia Nations) countries could be reduced significantly if proper alternatives to criminal justice proceedings were applied to their fullest potential.

"A Measure of Last Resort? Juvenile Justice in ASEAN Member States" is the first study of its kind and was presented as part of the official programme of the 13th UN Congress on Crime Prevention and Criminal Justice in Doha. The report provides statistical and narrative overviews of the juvenile justice situation and systems in all ASEAN countries.

"While the report confirms that there is a rise in juvenile crime in the region, it also finds that a remarkably low number of juveniles are in contact with the formal criminal justice system," said Christian Ranheim from RWI's Jakarta office.

The study presents, for the first time, statistics on the juvenile justice situation in the region, which show that each year 70,000 children are charged with a criminal offence in ASEAN countries. This is far less than in other comparable parts of the world. While this may be because of under-reporting of crimes, crime levels in South East Asia are low. It is reported that 16,000 juveniles below the age of 18 are deprived of their liberty in the region.

The study identifies several issues of common concern across member states, and RWI hopes it may lead to new initiatives and dialogue that may enhance the protection of children in conflict with the law in the ASEAN region. The report has been financed by Swedish Development Cooperation, under RWI's Regional Asia Programme, and carried out under the auspices of RWI's office in Jakarta.

B. Local Studies

The 2015 Philippines: Evaluation of the Intervention and Rehabilitation Program in Residential Facilities and Diversion Programs for Children in Conflict with the Law aimed to improve continuously the transparency and use of evaluation, UNICEF Evaluation Office manages the "Global Evaluation Reports Oversight System. " All the programs under evaluation are relevant in meeting the needs of CICL in the areas of health care, education, skills, security and safety, and spiritual and value formation. They are also relevant to the aim of bringing Philippine juvenile justice law and practice into compliance with international conventions. However, significant gaps still exist in meeting international conventions' rights protection standards. The full implementation of the Law, especially the diversion programs, and adequate compliance at the local level are not satisfactory.

Considerable evidence has shown that most programs provide an enabling environment for the rehabilitation and reintegration of CICL. Interviews with parents and children confirm changes in the behavior of the CICL in the programs. As almost all the facilities visited provide same services for CICL under sentence suspension, rehabilitation, intervention, and diversion, this evaluation cannot articulate the changes brought about by the different programs to CICL. Official statistics on the percentage of former CICL who go back to school or who find a job are unavailable. There is likewise no available empirical information on the recidivism rate of CICL who have taken part in the programs, as compared to those who have not.

Most of the programs visited by the evaluation team can meet the minimum ratio of CICL to social workers (15:1). In almost all the programs, social workers are also tasked with handling issues that are not related to CICL. Almost all program staff, regardless of their job titles as social workers or house parents, stated that the lack of training affects the efficiency of their work. Financial resources, like human resources, are quite stretched in the programs visited.

Intervention programs on juvenile delinquency by Kristine d. Aala, Jenie m. Ramos, Ruben Mendoza, Emerson Magnaye, Merwina Lou a. Bautista: This study aimed to determine the intervention programs on juvenile delinquency implemented by selected barangay in Batangas City. The study used the descriptive method of research and used a self-made questionnaire as the primary tool in gathering information. The respondents of this research were Brgy. officials of selected barangays in Batangas City. In terms of Physical and Health, the program that is highly implemented is the Clean and Green Program, while for education is the Free Education Program. Program on Material Recovery are perceived by most of the respondents as highly implemented regarding livelihood. In terms of the psychological, spiritual and development of on children in conflict with the law, it was found out that parent-child interaction program was the highest. The continuous implementation of the programs is recommended for the effective rehabilitation and restoration of child in conflict with the law. Utilization and improvement of other programs would also be substantial in developing the character and personality of these children.

This study is conceived by the researchers because the increasing number of juvenile delinquents bothered them based on the records of Batangas City Police Station. The researchers want to awaken the minds of barangay officials whose tasks are not only to supervise and organize their barangay but also to help children in conflict with the law with help rather than punishment.

Majority of the respondents are male, falls in the age bracket of 41 to 47 years old and mostly barangay councillor. In terms of Physical and Mental Health, the program that is highly implemented is the Clean and Green Program, while for education is the Free Education Program. Programs on Material Recovery are perceived by most of the respondents as highly implemented regarding livelihood. In terms of the psychological, spiritual and development of children in conflict with the law, it was found out that parent-child interaction program was the highest. Lack of constant monitoring of child in conflict with the law was the only problem observed.

Though there are various programs set by the government and non-government agencies, there is still a need to conduct regular assessments as to their applicability in meeting the needs of children in conflict with the law. Activities for the spiritual development of the child should be incorporated, as this aspect is lacking in the intervention programs employed. It is an important intervention to transform the total person of a child to become a God-fearing person. They should involve the community in efforts to protect children through the conduct of sufficient advocacy and awareness programs. There is a need to prepare a memorandum of agreement between implementing agencies to ensure their proper coordination and establish a common monitoring system covering the various stages of the juvenile justice process. Continuous implementation of these programs for the effective rehabilitation and restoration of juvenile delinquents furthermore utilization and improvement of other programs would also be substantial in developing the character and personality of these children. That future researchers conduct similar study to validate or dispute the findings of this study.

Research on the situation of children in conflict with the law in selected metro manila cities by *Adhikain Para sa Karapatang Pambata* Ateneo Human Rights Center: According to this research, diversion practice in the Philippines is limited by the following factors:

• ***The diversion procedure is limited in its scope***. Although diversion is provided only under the Rules on Juveniles in Conflict with the Law issued by the Supreme Court and only applicable to cases that reach the courts, diversion is widely practiced across all pillars. Officials from the community, law enforcement, prosecution and city social workers, practice diversion in one form or another unofficially since there are no guidelines, rules or law which provides for it, except for conciliation and mediation procedure in the community level provided under the *Katarungang*

Pambarangay Law. In these instances, only children whose cases fall under an official who practices unofficial diversion enjoy the benefit of diversion.

• ***Diversion under the Rules*** only covers offences where the maximum penalty imposed by law is imprisonment of not over six months. Because of this provision, only a few children are covered by diversion. As mentioned before, the common offences committed by children involve crimes against property, persons and drug-related offences, offences that are penalized by over six months. There are only a few offences wherein the law imposes imprisonment of not over six months, i.e., slight physical injuries, alarms and scandals, grave threats, unjust vexation, and possession of a deadly arrow. In addition, since the barangay conciliation system under the *Katarungang Pambarangay* Law already covers offences punished by imprisonment of one year or less, which includes the offences covered by diversion, only a few cases reach the courts. The barangay may have already successfully mediated the cases that are covered by diversion. As discussed in the chapter on observance of laws of the court and prosecution, there are Family Courts that apply the diversion process even though the case is not covered by diversion under the Rules.

• *Diversion under the Rules is limited to cases wherein the complaint or information is filed with the Family Courts*. In areas where there are no designated Family Courts, children in conflict with the law whose cases are filed in the Regional Trial Courts are excluded from availing of the benefits of diversion.

• *Diversion programme under the Rules may include community-based programmes or work-detail programmes in the community*. The choice of the Committee in designing a diversion programme may be limited since there is an absence of community-based programmes or work detailed programmes designed to address the needs of children in conflict with the law. Even though the creation of a BCPC has been encouraged since 1974, only a few barangays have established such and even if established, its effectivity is questioned. The communities and its officials need to receive sensitivity and skills training in dealing with children in conflict with the law.

• Under the Rules, the Committee may only recommend diversion if the complainant does not object thereto. When diversion is subjected to the consent of the complainant, there will be children unable to avail of it because of the desire of some complainants for revenge, punishment, or to teach the child a lesson by pushing for trial and/or imprisonment of the child. For example, there are department stores or malls which do not permit settlement of cases and have a policy of proceeding with the prosecution of cases, regardless of the amount of the item stolen, and even if the offender is a child.

Life after rehab: Experiences of discharged youth offenders with crime desistance by Pierce S. Docena: This study explored the experiences of former youth offenders regarding crime desistance. Guided by the life story method in research, the researcher interviewed ten male youth offenders who had been discharged from the Regional Rehabilitation Center for Youth (RRCY) in Eastern Visayas. The narratives of the research participants revealed that desistance from crime is a long and difficult process influenced by various factors such as family support, condition of one's community, intervention of significant persons, having a job, getting married, and having children. Implications for crime desistance studies are discussed and the challenges and opportunities for researchers and professionals who deal with youth offenders are likewise examined.

Spiritual Transformation of Imprisoned Boys in the Philippines by Marjon Junederbyshire: This thesis investigates and identifies processes of 'spiritual transformation' in rehabilitation programmes for boys from prison in the Philippines. Information was collected for this qualitative research by individual and group interviews and participant and non-participant observation in ten institutions during five weeks' fieldwork in the Philippines. Members of staff and resident boys were interviewed in jails and rehabilitation centres and some boys were visited in their homes.

The thesis argues that boys who suffer deprivation at home, on the streets and in jail become alienated from society. When events lead to an experience of spiritual awakening, the subsequent treatment they receive can either lead them to change their lives or it can thwart them from doing so. With encouragement, boys can merge positive life changes and reach a lasting condition of spiritual transformation.

The thesis shows how some programs of rehabilitation in the Philippines allow deprived children to experience and develop constructive relationships of trust, reliance, attachment and commitment, and how this assists the development of faith that is a significant component of spiritual transformation. The thesis shows how such programs catalyze and nurture this spiritual transformation.

This thesis contributes originally to knowledge in rehabilitation of Children in Conflict with the Law and the spiritual aspects of rehabilitation. It builds upon previous research in faith development and adds to this body of scholarship. Findings gained from this research can apply to policy elsewhere.

Intervention Programs for Children in Conflict with the Law (CICL): Gearing towards sustainable development: The Regional Juvenile Justice and Welfare Committee in Region 10 continuously performing its roles and functions in implementing Republic Act 9344 as amended. Strong partnership and collaboration with the coordinating agencies is frequently practiced and given importance to ensure effective and efficient delivery of technical help to the Local Government Units and other stakeholders. In view of the above premise, are highly recommended for the Local Government Units to make sure that RA 9344, as amended by RA 10630, will be fully implemented for the paramount interest of children. Massive campaign for information/awareness on children's right must be instituted to enhance community awareness on children's protection and development. The Local Project Monitoring Committee serves as the monitoring arm that is mandated to monitor all development projects of the municipality, while the Local Juvenile Justice Information System as mandated should be adopted by the municipality to update regularly the local profile of CICL and CAR. The program design contains strategies that are relevant and responsive to the diverse needs of CICL and CAR population.

Justification of the Study

One of the major problems of youth today is juvenile delinquency in society. Murder, rape, motor vehicle theft, robbery, aggravated assault, larceny, arson, and burglary are acts of violence that are steadily rising because of juveniles taking part in committing these acts of violence. As years continue to pass, there has been an enormous concern of how parents, police, counselors, teachers, and friends feel that the ability to control or stop juvenile acts of violence is slowly slipping away over time and are desperately trying to alter behavioral patterns that continue into these dangerous ways of life.

Before I attempted to determine the cause for this specific phenomenon, consideration has to be given to the area of location, background of an individual, family pattern, and life at home as these variables affect how a child is raised and how they react to violence. Because of the different theoretical orientations, I could understand and assess the situation of these children who who are in conflict with the law. According to the classical conditioning of Ivan Pavlov, the CICL were conditioned by the environment with a new stimulus which resulted delinquent behaviors. Based on the theory of Erik Erikson the age 12 to 18 years old are the most vulnerable to be influenced by the environment because they are on the stage of ego identity vs role confusion. Since most of the CICL were influenced by their peers and their environment, the social learning of Albert Bandura strengthens the assessment that this model are huge influencers to the behavior of the child. This influenced where strengthened by the Family System Theory of Dr. Bowen wherein the family relationship shows major impact on the child's behavior because of the system pattern of dynamics of relationship. According to B.F. Skinner, punishment is an ineffective way of controlling behaviour, leading to short-term behaviour. These behavioral theories have been synthesized to guide me in my reflections on lived experiences.

Therefore, as a social worker, strength-based approach is an appropriate intervention in helping these children. This will be instrumental in successfully shifting the balance of care and develop services that are focused on prevention and independence. This will also challenge social services' historical focus on clients' deficiencies to a focus on possibilities and solutions In effect, the strengths perspective is the social work equivalent in emphasize the origins of strength and resilience and argue against the dominance of a problem-focused perspective. This should help society get a better feel of the negative behavioral patterns and thoughts of our children and should hopefully change the way future generations carry out their everyday lives.

The review related studies and literature focused on the current issues facing by the CICL. There is an increase in the number of children passing through criminal justice systems and still charging children to a criminal offense in the ASEAN Countries. In the Philippines, among the priority bills of President Duterte and his allies in Congress is the lowering of the minimum age of criminal responsibility (MACR) from 15 to 9 years old although there are limited infrastructure, facilities and diversion program guidelines that deprived children to experience and develop constructive relationships of trust, reliance, attachment and commitment.

Despite of these issues, the UNICEF, together with the government and non-government organizations, are exerting effort to evaluate the gaps about implementing the law. Enhanced programs and services were piloted from different NGO's such as holistic development programs, transformational programs, and spiritual development programs.

I focus my study on the lived experiences of children in conflict with the law towards their journey of transformation and to find out the contributing factors of the Manila Youth Reception Center on their narratives. In this study, I integrated the theories of Ivan Pavlov, B.F. Skinner, Erik Erikson, and Albert Bandura to better understand the lived experiences of the children in conflict with the law.

In this study, I am guided by the application of the integral approach, through exploring and understanding their lived experiences:

- I explored the world of the inner self of my co-researchers, including personal thoughts, feelings, intuitions, and values/meanings.
- I explored the shared world of meanings within groups and cultures and much of their meaning is generated and conveyed through language. Fields such as hermeneutics, semiotics, history, anthropology, and religious studies further explained this inter-subjective realm.
- I take an external or "aim" approach, wherein I also focused on unexplored and gave focus on systems involving the lived experiences of my co-researchers' journey toward awakening their compassion. I focused on meanings and other inner experiences that emerged from such collectives, and described their characteristics and mechanisms as viewed from without.

This study also explores what the virtue of the lived experiences of my co-researchers can offer for both the profession and practice of Social Work.

Chapter III

METHODOLOGY

In this chapter, I present the method of my study. I explain the research approach I used in my study, selection of my co-researchers, ways of gathering lived experiences, manner of analyzing the lived experiences, and the process doing my phenomenological study.

My Research Approach

The approach I used in my study is phenomenology. By the principles of phenomenology, I explored the meanings and what new understandings from the lived experiences of Children in Conflict with the Law from Manila Youth Reception Center as influenced by the particular context within which they are occurring.

The phenomenological approach aims to describe a particular phenomenon reflectively to draw meaningful and essential insights–of a phenomenon under investigation and the theoretical and practical implications of the eidetic insight. Here the participants of the study–my co-researchers and I–shared our lived experiences of the degree by which we are fully conscious of the essence of our work–which is our awakening to ourselves towards transformative impact of the different programs and services provided.

The Philosophical Foundation of Phenomenology

Edmund Husserl, a German philosopher (1859-1938) laid the foundation of the phenomenological movement as a way of doing philosophy. His philosophy is based on the belief that reality is intentional, that humans direct their consciousness towards object. Husserl defines phenomenology as the reflective study of the essence of consciousness as experienced from the first-person point of view (Smith, 2007). Phenomenology promotes an understanding of the relationship between states of individual consciousness and social life. It seeks to reveal how human awareness is being inferred from the production of social action, social situation and social worlds. In phenomenology, bracketing approach is used in investigating from a meaning context in the common-sense world; will all judgments suspended (Bentz, 1995).

Husserl believed that a sharp contrast exists between facts and essences, between the real and non-real. He asserted that, "Essence provides on the one side a knowledge of the essential nature of the Real, on the other, regarding the domain left over, knowledge of the essential nature of the non-real" (1931, p.45). The transformation of individual or empirical experience into essential insight occurs through a special process that Husserl calls "ideation" (Kockelmans, 1967, p.80). The object that appears in consciousness mingles with the object in nature so that a meaning is created, and knowledge is extended. Thus, a relationship exists between what exists in conscious awareness and what exists in the world. What appears in consciousness is an absolute reality, while what appears in the world is a product of learning.

While Husserl was in the realm of Epistemology that answers the question of what it is to know (Epistemology), his famous student, Martin Heidegger, an existential phenomenologist, focused on "beingness" (Ontology). Both authors focused on two movements in the human person: 1) intentionality: we are absorbed by the world outside us., 2) reflexivity: a capacity to go back to oneself, a going inward, and reflect on the meaning to us of the phenomenon we are preoccupied about.

Stephan Strasser, phenomenology is a well-known for his synthesis of the various points of view about phenomenology. He says that phenomenology is hermeneutic, intuitive and dialect. Hermeneutic means interpretive. It seeks to look at reality from the set of meaning of the observer. The intuitive looks into insight. It deals with the meaning that people give. Dialectic views reality from different angles or points for confirming, checking, and changing the information. Through a phenomenological approach, I could get a deep and entire description of human experiences and meaning. Insights do not come from the researcher himself, but also from the product of the interactive process between researcher and those who provide for the information.

Practitioners of Phenomenology in Human and Social Science

Mina M. Ramirez was the first in the Philippines to use the phenomenological method in social science, particularly in Sociology, way back in 1966 in her master's thesis in ASI, A Phenomenology of the Filipino Family. The phenomenological method was asked by a national organization in Social Science, known as The Baguio Religious Acculturation Conference (BRAC) to be presented in its Eleventh Annual Conference, 1967 (St. Louis Quarterly, 1968). In all her articles on phenomenology, she describes this as a human approach based on lived experiences. According to her, phenomenology is to discover the system of values and social structures as these are living in a person in society.

Dr. Ramirez added that "phenomenology is the primary method of inquiry, which, as she explains, does not make use of empirical tools such as questionnaires or any other scientific apparatus." Thus, it is also referred as the "method of the encounter." This is because the individual considers the object of study not as pure object-subject that can be known through "inter-subjectivity." This study enabled me to validate inter-subjectivities from my experiences and the life experiences of my co-researchers. She stated that what appears from our conventional senses has to be reflected upon in a series of reflections to uncover layers of consciousness. The explanation is sensed and grasped from a second level of reflection (a second level of consciousness) and a series of reflections or consciousness levels.

Clark Moustakas, another social practitioner, explains the nature, meanings, and essence of Epoche, Phenomenological Reduction, Imaginative Variation, and synthesis necessary in order to conduct phenomenological research. He considers phenomenology as a significant method as he developed it, for investigating human experience and for deriving knowledge from a state of pure consciousness. One learns to see naively and freshly again, to value conscious experience, to respect the evidence of one's senses, and to move toward an inter-subjective knowing of things, people, and everyday experiences (Moustakas, 1994).

In this approach, I did not submit myself to write all existing theories to help explain the phenomenon. Instead, I gave more attention to the primary experiences of my co-researchers as the basis of my insight formulation. Because of the culled social facts, I view the phenomenon from our experiences.

In phenomenology, I entered a "transcendental sphere." I derived the eidetic reduction from the Greek word "*eidos*" which means essence. In this study, I reduced the experience to its essence.

Selection of My Co-Researchers

My co-researchers are children in conflict with the law from Manila Youth Reception Center. I will purposely choose six CICL as my co-researchers base on my following criteria:

- Male
- 16 to 18 years old
- Rehabilitated in MYRC for 1 year
- Currently immersed/reintegrated in their community for 1 year
- Has expressed willingness to cooperate in the study

My Co-Researchers

Table 2. Our Profile

Co-researcher	Name	Age	Sex	Educ. Att.	Case	Years of Admission in MYRC	Years of Reintegrated in the community
1	"John Paul"	17	M	Grade 9	R.A. 9165 Sec 11 Art 11	2017-2018	2019-2020
2	"Aga"	17	M	Grade 11	R.A. 9165 Sec 11 Art 11	2017-2018	2019-2020
3	"Jaja"	17	M	Grade 9	R.A. 9165 Sec 5 Art 11	2017-2018	2019-2020
4	"Jashtin"	16	M	Grade 6	R.A. 9165 Sec 11 Art 11	2018-2019	2019-2020
5	"Jay"	17	M	Grade 8	R.A. 9165 Sec 11 Art 11	2017-2018	2018-2020
6	"Gerald"	16	M	Grade 7	R.A. 9165 Sec 11 Art 11	2017-2019	2019-2020
7	"JR"		M	BSSW	Social Worker / Researcher		

Ways of Gathering Lived Experiences

Narrative writing (story telling): Given a set of unstructured questionnaire guide for them to write their narrative stories about their lived experiences (see attached appendix A). Narratives differ from answers because my co-researchers choose and order the relevant issues through telling and relate the details into the context. Narratives have the point, the plot, and temporal structure. Narrative information provides active social facts to the sensitive issues and topics that are difficult to grasp through questioning.

Practitioners have used narrative writing to help explain strengths of individuals and communities. Practitioners using this approach assume that hidden inside any 'problem' narrative is a story of strength and resilience. This will often require re-framing of the situation to highlight any unique instances of strengths into a story of resilience.

They found the practice of narrative on the principle that people live their lives by stories or narratives that they have created through their experiences, and which then shapes their further life experience. A key part of this approach recognizes that some people may think of a problem as an integral part of their character. Separating this problem from the person by externalizing it allows them to deal with it constructively (Epston and White, 1992).

Unstructured in-depth Interview: This is a systematic way of talking and listening to my co-researchers and another way of gathering lived experiences through conversations. I used open-ended questions and unstructured interview wherein I have a list of topics for my co-researchers to talk about like "What are their lived experiences on their journey as children in conflict with the law" but are free to rc-phrase the questions as they wish. They are free to answer in any way they choose.

Interviewing is a way to collect social facts and to gain knowledge from my co-researchers. Interviews are ways for my co-researchers to get involved and talk about their views. In addition, they can discuss their perception and interpretation regarding a situation. It is their expression from their point of view. I need to know and select the method for addressing the needs of the research question. Then, I need to decide and choose the right method for this study.

This narrative is a pervasive structure with which I comprehend and convey the experiences and meanings of events. It is an account of my own and others' behaviour, revealing myself to others in how I would like to be seen. In doing so, I will also reveal something of the structure of my social world. For these reasons, the stories that my co-researchers tell provide me important information about their experience in relation to identity and social life. I will provide a structured approach to conducting narrative analysis that accounts for how my co-researchers position themselves through telling stories to an audience in a broader social life. This is an approach through narrative that integrates personal and social stories which is very useful in this study to understand the phenomenon of the lived experiences of CICL in Manila Youth Reception Center..

Art-Symbolism: Using art as a method to gather their lived experiences, my co-researchers applied their creativity thru arts. I asked my co-researchers to draw a symbol that can be best explained their lived experiences. This method will allow my co-researchers to use the exploration of personal symbols in the art-making process to find personal meaning. Through the production of a body of artwork that features visual metaphors and personal symbols, understanding of the self as an individual can be achieved. This discovery can transcend my co-researchers into a new realm of self-discovery and communication with others. This method of collecting additional information was very helpful in analyzing the lived experiences deeper and can validate their stories from the narrative writing and interview results.

Ethical Considerations

In this study, I did not use research procedure that may harm my co-researchers either physically or psychologically. I am also obligated at all times to use the least stressful research procedure. When harm seems inevitable, I must find other means of obtaining the information or to abandon the research. Instances may rise in which exposing the child to stressful conditions may be necessary if diagnostic or therapeutic benefits to the child are associated with the study.

Before seeking consent or assent from my co-researchers, I informed them of all features of the study that may affect their willingness to take part and should answer their questions in terms appropriate to their comprehension. I respected the freedom to choose to take part in the research or not by giving them the opportunity to give or not give assent to participation and to choose to discontinue participation.

To gain access to institutional records, I got permission from responsible authorities in charge of records. Anonymity of the information is preserved, and no information used other than that for which I got permission. It is my responsibility to ensure that responsible authorities do, in fact, have the confidence and that they bear some responsibility in giving such permission. In complying with requirements for information sharing, I carefully consider whether they have provided information which, if combined, risks violating participant anonymity.

I keep in confidence all information got about my co-researchers. My co-researchers identity is concealed in written and verbal reports of the results, as well as in informal discussion with students and colleagues. When a possibility exists that others may gain access to such information, this possibility, together with the plans for protecting confidentiality, should be explained to the participants as part of the procedure of obtaining informed consent.

Process of Doing Phenomenology

Step 1: Gathering of Lived Experiences with "epoche" as an attitude: The first step which I refrained myself from judgment, to abstain from and stay away from ordinary way of perceiving the phenomenon. In this step, it requires me a new way of looking at things, a way that requires me to learn to see what stands before my eyes, and what I can distinguish and describe. In this step, I set aside my everyday understandings, judgments, and knowing so that I can revisit the phenomena freshly, naively, with a wide open sense, from the vantage point of a pure and transcendental ego. +

During this step, I applied and facilitated different ways of gathering lived experiences. I conducted in-depth interview to each co-researcher based on their available schedule. I interview them in a venue where they can openly discuss their inner self and assure comfortability for the one whole day session. I used open-ended questions and unstructured interview wherein I have a list of topics for my co-researchers to talk about like "What are their experiences in their journey being children in conflict with the law" but are free to phrase the questions as they wish. They are free to answer in any way they choose. After the interview session, I asked my co-researchers to draw a symbol that their life experiences can describe and give them an opportunity to discuss and talk about their personal meaning of the phenomenon. This method allowed me to visualize easily their experiences and validate their narratives.

Since I also used the naturalistic and field studies technique as a way of gathering social facts, I visited their community monthly to observe my co-researchers in their life routine where I can get a better look at their behavior of interest as they occur in the real-world. This allows me to notice new ideas and social facts not stated during the interview. Such observations can serve as an inspiration for further validation of the gathered social facts.

According to the principle of analysis of phenomenological approach is to use an emergent strategy to allow the method of analysis to follow the nature of the social facts itself. This stage is the start of the entire process of collecting narratives and art symbols based on the lived experiences of my six co-researchers, including my story. The common theme of each story was formulated based on the lived experiences as shared by my co-researchers. I internalized their stories and made sure they were documented fully. Correction, clarification and validation of their stories are properly facilitated. The artistic depictions of experience were approached differently. In all cases, the focus was on an understanding of the meaning of the description.

Step 2: ***First Reflection***: ***Textual Themes***: I considered the singularity of experiences of my co-researchers. The phenomenon is perceived and described in its totality, in a fresh and open way. It helps me to provide a complete description given by its essential constituents, variations of perceptions, thoughts, feelings, sounds, color, and shapes. Ultimately, through this step, textural themes or meaning units from the narratives/stories will be drawn out.

Step 3: ***Imaginative Variation-Structural Themes***: This step leads me to grasp the structural essence of my co-researchers' experiences. I used my intellect to assist my imagination, sense, and memory to intuit distinctly and to unite correctly what is sought after with what is known in order that the former may be distinguished. This step helps me to arrive at a structural differentiation among the infinite multiplicities of actual and cognitions that relate to the object in question and thus can somehow go together to make up the unity of an identifying synthesis.

I continued the second reflection on how the lived experiences of my co-researchers resonated with my understanding and feelings. I clustered the themes and identified the overall theme of each cluster. The overall theme of each cluster provided the basis for the clustering. This is the structural theme. I went beyond the words to the context of "given with" the narrative or art. However, I did not interpret excessively. If the meaning was not clear, I did not read the description of the experience beyond the clear meaning. In this study, I used collective themes that occur across the group of participants.

Step 4: ***Synthesis of Meanings and Essence–Postulates/Essential Insights and Eidetic Insight***: The last step in the phenomenological research process is the intuitive integration of the fundamental textural and structural descriptions into essential insights or postulates. The essential insights/postulates will make up the elements of a unified statement of the essence (eidetic insight) of the experience of the phenomenon. Translating into Art Form their stories will bring about imagery the narratives with the underlying meaning of these. The main researcher created composite art forms. In this step, I will give highlight about my creative synthesis and possibilities.

Symbolic Representation of My Study

The symbolic representation of my phenomenological process is "***Game over***" "sign, which is a message in video games that signals to the player that the game has ended. Usually, the connotes a negative meaning when continued play is disallowed, such as losing all of one's lives or failing a critical aim; sometimes it is positive when a game is completed successfully. Each step symbolized resembles how I processed my phenomenological study. I connected each step in a similar way that I described and understood the lived experiences of children in conflict with the law. I applied intuitive inquiry that led me into a new eidetic insight or wisdom that inspires and awakens the consciousness of a compassionate delivery of service interventions to the society for children in conflict with the law. I present below the symbolic representation of my phenomenological process.

Figure 2: Symbolic Representation of my Phenomenological Process

This phenomenological approach is very much aligned with me because it is guided by Epoche, phenomenological reduction, imaginative variation, and a synthesis of meanings and essence. For me, this has been a natural process through which awareness, understanding, and knowledge are derived from the lived experiences of CICL from MYRC.

Figure 3: 'GAME OVER' Sign

It starts with consciousness awakening of my co-researchers through the application of different ways of gathering social facts such as narrative writing, in-depth interview and art symbolism. I symbolized it in a game over sign wherein they need to open up and extract their experiences related to their journey of being a child in conflict with the law. They recalled their experiences during their past journey and lead to transformational phenomenon of the impact of the program and services of MYRC.

Figure 4: Continue Sign

On the second phase of my symbolic representation is the '**continue**' button. I symbolize this as the combination of different social facts from diverse perspectives and experiences of my co-researchers. Themes are analyzed and the first reflection from our journey is revealed. I continue to symbolize by moving forward to another level. This is similar to the process of my phenomenological study where I continue to go to a deeper understanding of the lived experiences of my co-researchers.

In the third phase, the '**start**' button is the symbol. In the phenomenological process, this is my **structural themes**. After the '**continue**' button, a new game may be started. In the phenomenological process, after identifying the **extracted textual themes**, I created new themes, which are the structural themes. This is a deeper reflection which is leading to the essence and meaning of our lived experiences.

Figure 5: Start a new game

Lastly, I symbolize the eidetic insight with a '**new game**'. Children's minds are not yet fully developed, they are less mature. They have a harder time understanding the consequences of their actions, and they are vulnerable to peer pressure. As a result, we recognize them to have a perspective of life as a game that they usually play.

Figure 6: New game begins

The phenomenological process helped my co-researchers go back and reflect on their journey. Their heart had softened; their minds and opinions changed; and they learned new perspectives from their lived experiences. The entire purpose of this study is to look into the opportunity given to the CICL to learn from their mistakes without being overly focused on the consequences.

The program of Juvenile System is about giving CICLs a second chance and creating a healthier community for them. The opportunities that arise when someone can take ownership of an offense can still be accepted into the community help to build confidence as a sense of appreciation in these children.

This phenomenological process is not just about enhancing the programs and services of juvenile system; it is also about bringing the community together to understand the lived experiences of CICL and to help in the restoration process.

Chapter IV

REFLECTIVE NARRATIVES, THEMATIC REFLECTIONS AND EIDETIC INSIGHT

This chapter presents our lived-experiences, i.e., my story as the researcher and the respective stories of former residents of Manila Youth Reception Center (MYRC) who have been reintegrated with their families and communities.

In our respective story, a first reflection is provided. I culled important themes from our stories. Said themes are the highlights of our experiences that were distilled from our narratives. Common feelings, experiences and perceptions were well distilled, thus leading to identify the important themes.

Next is the second reflection, followed by the eidetic insight of the study. Subsequently, this is synthesized to get the essence of our stories. Validation is done by referring to the related literature and studies reviewed. Subsequently, I analyzed the study and came up with various insights taken from the lived experiences.

Socio-Demographic Profile of My Co-Researchers

Six former residents from Manila Youth Reception Center were reintegrated with their respective families and communities. They were willing enough to share their stories. Their age range is 16–17 years old. All are currently in high school. They are all Catholics and all have committed crime under R.A. 9165 Sec 11 Art 11.

Our Stories, Our Journey

Each journey of my co-researchers, including mine, is contained in our respective story which is presented below. The respective journey of my co-researchers has a corresponding written self-report and symbolism of their experiences.

Co-Researcher 1

"A Struggle towards Climbing to the Peak of Success"

"My name is John Paul, second child in a brood of five. I could reach Grade 9, and was studying in a public school near our house. My parents are both hardworking; my father is a security guard in a private company in Manila, while my mother tends a small sari-sari store in our house. My mother wanted to earn to augment my father's income, so she could have emergency funds and enough money for other expenses. Despite this, my mother never neglected us. She takes care of our needs while tending to her sari-sari store. She maintained cleanliness and orderliness inside our house. She teaches us with our home works and lessons. She teaches us values and always gives us pieces of advice. She is the first to reprimand us whenever we commit mistakes. She is generous in complimenting us for a job well done. Our life is simple. We have a home to shield us from the heat, rain, and strong winds. We have clothes on our backs. We can study and can eat nutritious and delicious food three times a day.

Our lives changed when my father died. He died when I was in grade 7. A group of armed men forcibly entered the building where my father was working. One of the armed men shot him. According to the cops who responded and who immediately brought him to the nearest hospital, my father was already dead by the time they arrived. His death was a significant loss for us all because he was a role model to us all. He had no vices and most of all, we all knew and felt how much he loved my mother and us. Though tired from work, he never failed to give quality time for us, for our mother.

When my father died, my mother did her best to provide all our needs. The money she got from my father's death was used as an additional income in her small sari-sari store. While we slowly recovered from my father's death, I was left behind, still grieving over the loss of my father.

I still could not accept my father's death, much to my detriment. I still miss him to this day. I miss how he used to teach me with my lessons or homework. I miss the nights when we used to talk about his life in the province when he was still young. I miss the small pep talks, how he always told us to study hard because that is the only thing he and my mother could impart to us that can never be taken by other people. He used to tell us to always be kind to other people, and to always see the good in others. He never let other people abuse our kindness. He used to say, "Hangga't kaya ko kayong paaralin, papag-aralin ko kayo hanggang sa makapagtapos kayo. Ang hiling lang namin ng nanay ninyo ay magsipag kayo sa pag-aaral."

Instead of using my father's words to inspire me to persevere and overcome the grief and loneliness, and instead of studying harder so I could fulfill my dead father's dream for me, I drowned myself in grief, loneliness and longing for my father. I spiraled into a life so different from the one I used to live, a life that led me to commit offenses, which I regretted later on.

It started a couple of days after my father died. I used to go with my older sister in going to school every morning but this time; they forced me to go to school. After the prodding of my mother saying we can no longer afford to be absent because we already missed a couple of lessons when my father died, I finally went to school with a heavy heart and loneliness I could not contain. I'd rather sleep and cry all day; but I opted not to share my emotions with my mother and my siblings for fear that they may not understand me. I fear they might react differently, and they might say I should have gotten over it by now. Most of all, I did not want them to know I was still grieving over the loss of my father. I didn't want them to worry about me. I didn't want their pity, and I didn't want to be an additional burden to my mother. I didn't want anyone to know about how I feel. My decision to such brought me more suffering than I can imagine.

I was minding my business one morning inside the classroom when I saw some of my classmates, those who always cut classes. They are the students my late father warned me about. I can still hear his voice when he told me not to associate with those kinds of students. When my father was still alive, I paid them no heed. I never talked to them because I was focused on fulfilling my father's wish and I was determined to finish my studies without getting into any trouble. But that was ages ago. As I was not feeling too keen on listening to my teachers, I walked up to them to ask what they're doing the rest of the day. I thought to myself, maybe, just maybe, if I hang out with a different crowd, I may cope up better. The pain might ease up a bit and I may get back on my feet before I knew it. Carlo, the leader of the gang, greeted me and asked me what I wanted. I told him I wanted to hang out, and they all gave me a suspecting look. I told them I was not interested in the succeeding classes and I just wanted to "chill."

Most of the students in our school, hanging out with Carlo and his gang, meant getting into trouble once in a while, and cutting classes most of the time. For me, it meant escape from reality. My mother and siblings thought I was getting by. They thought I was slowly accepting my father's death, and that I was doing okay, but they were so wrong. They did not know I was continually spiraling deeper into a world so different from the one I used to know; I was living a life which was the exact opposite of the life I once had.

I learned to drink and smoke cigarettes because of Carlo and his gang. I learned to pilfer cigarettes and alcoholic beverages from small sari-sari stores whenever we wanted to drink. But, I did not have money to buy alcohol and cigarettes. I was always with Carlo and his gang. I never took notice of how much time had passed. After some time, we grew tired of drinking and smoking and stealing cigarettes and alcoholic beverages from small sari-sari stores. Carlo hatched an idea. He told us it would be fun to steal stuff inside houses, to actually go inside other people's homes and take valuable stuff and sell it or pawn it. Was I apprehensive? Of course I was, because not only did I know it was wrong, I also knew very well that we could go to jail if we get caught. I was already thinking of what mother would say if she found out. I was also thinking, if my father were alive, I would definitely get scolded, or worse, punished. I thought my father was a security guard who died doing his job, and here I am, on the brink of becoming the thief who shot him. Then again, my father is already dead, I thought. If we don't get caught the first time, I will never repeat what we're about to do.

When Carlo planned the whole thing, he did not say that we were actually going to do it. I was nervous, of course, and it was difficult for me to just go inside houses and take all their stuff. But the cash flow was good, and soon I owned good stuff-expensive clothes and shoes, a nice cellphone which I only use when I am in school (I didn't want anyone in my family to be suspicious), and cash, probably more cash than my mother ever earned in her small store. Although I knew my mother was already wondering where I got the money to buy all my expensive clothes and shoes I had, she did not dare ask me. I made sure I checked all the pockets of my clothes before I gave them to my mother during laundry day. She knew nothing about the new me – the drinking, smoking me, that forcibly enters other people's houses and steal stuff. I barely passed my subjects, but I managed because I made it a point to report to school during periodic examinations.

Although my grades plummeted to the lowest, I was still thankful that they did not expel me because of absences and tardiness. My adviser and I had a heart to heart talk; she gave me pieces of advice, and told me that if I ever needed someone to talk to, all I had to do was look for her in the faculty room. But I was too proud to seek help. No, I was too proud to admit I even needed help. I did not talk to her, or look for her even when I felt too low, or even on days when I sorely missed my father. Instead of heading to the faculty room to look for my adviser, I just urged Carlo and the gang to cut classes and go some place to relax.

While we were drinking and smoking marijuana (we became bored with just cigarettes), Carlo once again came up with a very brilliant idea that instead of just ransacking houses to buy marijuana, we should just peddle Shabu and marijuana. He explained selling prohibited drugs is going to be more dangerous, but more profitable. I no longer thought twice. I just went with the plan. We started tiny, a couple of grams of Shabu, a couple of sticks of marijuana a day. We sold them to college students at a university near our school, and because of this, I skipped school more than usual. Heck, I even skipped periodic examinations because we were so engrossed with selling prohibited drugs. They particularly overwhelmed me with the vast amount of money that I could take home. Sometimes I was tempted to give some money to my mother, to compensate for all my mistakes and offenses, but I knew mother will surely be suspicious if I gave her even a small amount.

Months went by so fast. We continued selling prohibited drugs wherever they were needed–schools, gyms, bars and clubs, depressed communities, subdivisions, and even in some government agencies. Little did we know we were already under surveillance The cops were on our trail, and they were preparing a buy-bust operation. One sunny afternoon, a man texted Carlo to ask if he has drugs available for pickup near the city hall. The mysterious texter, a huge transaction, ordered two (2) kilograms, even for Carlo. I told him not to take the texter seriously because his order was too big. I did not know Carlo had something else in mind. He asked me to meet the mysterious texter at the agreed time and place and to bring only a kilogram of what he needs. He said I could have 50% of the total revenue of that transaction. I was ecstatic. After giving me the merchandise, he told me where to go and I immediately set off. I only had an hour to travel and to ensure that I will not get caught while the merchandise was still in my possession.

When I arrived at the meeting place, I did not know who I was supposed to meet. I thought of calling Carlo when a man walked up to me and asked if I was John Paul. He then asked for the package, which I immediately gave him. He handed me the payment for the prohibited drugs. As I was about to put the money inside my pockets, the man who paid for the prohibited drugs suddenly put out a pair of handcuffs and started speaking while he was cuffing me. I had no chance to run. Everything happened so fast. The next thing I knew, I was inside a police station, being interviewed by a lady cop. I asked her if I could call my mother. She said, yes! She gave me my phone back. While waiting for my mother, I asked the lady cop if I'll be staying inside the police station for a long time. She said 'no' because they will transfer me to MYRC, an institution for Children-In-Conflict with the Law.

When my mother arrived at the police station, my adviser accompanied her. They talked about coincidence. My adviser paid my mother a visit to our house. They were in the middle of a discussion about my behavior in school when I called up my mother. She said she had become worried when I stopped going to school altogether, and that mother failed to report to school after they summoned her twice. I will forever remember my mother's face when she visited me inside the police station. She was crying her heart out and no one could understand what she was trying to say in between sobs. My adviser accompanying her to the police station made it worse. My mother asked me what happened, but I no longer replied. I became teary-eyed. The lady cop explained to my mother everything that she explained to me. We were told a social worker will handle my case in coordination with a public attorney.

When I arrived in MYRC, I was introduced to the social worker who will handle my case. She explained the rules and regulations inside MYRC, and the corresponding sanctions for every violation. She also told us the charge filed against me, and the measures which my mother and I can take for my welfare and best interest.

My first few weeks inside MYRC were the hardest. I had a hard time sleeping with so many teenagers inside the same small room with me; I was not used to waking up so early in the morning; most of all, I was not used to not seeing my mother often, or for only a couple of hours a week. Even my younger siblings could not visit me inside the institution because minors are not allowed inside. As the days progressed, I became better acquainted with my new environment. As I came to accept my fate, and that I might spend a long time in this institution, I learned to be friendly to the other CICLs inside the center.

I was fortunate that my social worker was nice, just like my adviser. He kept on reminding me to always behave and that I should do my best not to violate any rules and regulations of the center. He had such an impact on my life and became a beneficial influence on me. Whenever he had the opportunity, he would take me out; he talked to me often and told me I could talk to him whenever I needed someone to talk to. He even went to the extent of talking to my public attorney so that I may be allowed to go home and be with my mother and siblings during the holiday season. He vouched I was behaving well inside the center, even when I was not. My heart filled with hope as days turned into months. The prospect of not only seeing my family during the holiday season (Christmas until New Year) but spending it with them made me realize how much I missed them.

For the government, I hope they develop other programs for CICLs like me. I hope they could give us ample opportunities so that we can prove to society that CICLs can become better individuals and that we can change for the better. I also hope that one day CICLs and PDLs alike could lead normal lives again, without being judged by other people, without being stigmatized and treated like persons with a contagious disease.

My social worker said there are companies offering jobs to CICLs like me; however, these are only part-time employment and no guarantee. I wish that the government could provide permanent employment to CICLs and PDLs after they are released from detention.

Lastly, I also hope that government agencies such as TESDA and other similar agencies would provide technical and vocational skills to CICLs like me, even when we are still inside the institution for CICLs. My social worker told me that before, MYRC used to offer skills training programs; but these were limited to female wards, such as cooking and baking, sewing and basic hair cutting, but none was available to male wards. I hope that someday, skills training program will be made available to all CICLs to better prepare them before they are integrated into their families and communities.

My experience as a CICL was difficult because I brought pain and shame to my family, most especially to my mother, who has sacrificed so much and who has worked so hard since my father's death. My inability to cope with the loss of my father has caused me to neglect my studies, and worse, made me commit offenses that I now regret. Being a CICL was a regrettable experience; but inside the MYRC, I discovered myself. While I suffer day after day inside the institution, the people I considered friends are still out there, doing the things we used to do. They never cared to visit me, or bothered to send food or medicine when I was sick. I realized they were with me only in times of enjoyment, but they left the minute I was apprehended. While inside the institution, I also realized that there are people who could help me, if only I would allow them to, just like when my adviser offered me some help, but I refused. I learned that these have to start with me.

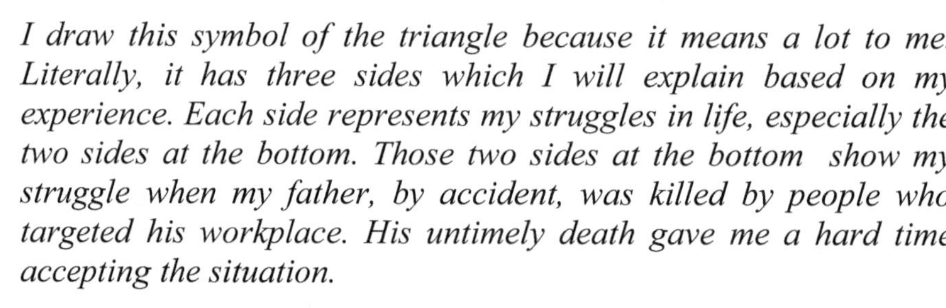

Figure 7: Triangle Symbol

I draw this symbol of the triangle because it means a lot to me. Literally, it has three sides which I will explain based on my experience. Each side represents my struggles in life, especially the two sides at the bottom. Those two sides at the bottom show my struggle when my father, by accident, was killed by people who targeted his workplace. His untimely death gave me a hard time accepting the situation.

Raised by my father's love, affection and guidance makes me feel alone and I struggle too much in life. Even though my mother did her very best to give everything to us, I must be honest that I'm longing to my father. I have tried to move on but every time I remember my father it hurts me a lot, especially because there was no justice to his death. My mother also tries to be strong but I can see her hardship in life. I must adore my family because they keep pushing for my enlightenment. They motivate me to continue my life without my father. They believe that someday I will surpass this tragic situation and will climb to the peak of the triangle which means to me that I will be successful in life. This triangle, although it has only three sides, each sides has its own meaning. Reaching the top is the most challenging one."

First Reflection: Textual Themes

1 I have responsible and hardworking parents who never neglected us and generous in complementing us for a job well done.

2 Our lives changed when my father died, his death was a great loss because he was a role model to us all.

3 I was left behind still grieving the loss of my father, and I still could not accept my father's death.

4 My parents always told us to study hard because that is the only thing they could impart to us

5 I drowned myself in grief, loneliness and longing for my father

6 A life that led me to commit offenses which I regretted later on

7 I entered the school with a heavy heart and a loneliness I could not contain

8 I opted not to share my emotions to my family for fear that they may not understand me

9 If I hang out with a different crowd, I may be able to cope up better, the pain might easy up a bit and I may be able to get back on my feet

10 I was not interested in the succeeding classes and I just wanted to relax

11 Hanging with the gang means escaping from reality

12 I was living a life which that was the exact opposite of the life I once had

13 I know it was wrong, I also know very well that we could go to jail if we get caught

14 I was nervous and it as not easy for me to just go inside houses and take all their stuff

15 I barely passed my subjects but thankful I was not expelled because of absences and tardiness

16 My adviser and I had a heart to heart talk and she give me pieces of advice

17 Selling prohibited drugs is going to be more dangerous but more profitable

18 I skipped school more than usual, because we were engrossed with selling prohibited drugs

19 I was tempted to give more money to my mother, to compensate for all my mistakes and offenses

20 I had no chance to run, everything happened so fast

21 I will forever remember my mother's face when she visited me inside the police station

22 My first few weeks inside MYRC were the hardest, I had a hard time sleeping with so many teenagers inside the same small room

23 I became better acquainted with my new environment

24 I learned to be friendly to the other CICLs inside the center

25 I was fortunate that my social worker is nice and he had such an impact in my life.

26 My heart began to fill with hope, as days turned into months realizing how I miss my family so much

27 Give us ample opportunities to prove to society that we are capable of becoming better individuals and have the ability to change for the better

28 CICLs and PDLs alike would be able to lead normal lives again, without being

judged by other people, without being stigmatized and being treated like persons with a contagious disease.

29 Provide permanent employment to CICLs and PDL after they are leased from detention

30 Provide technical and vocational skills for male wards to better prepare them before they are integrated to their families and communities

31 I brought pain and shame to my family, most especially to my mother who has sacrificed so much.

32 My inability to cope with the loss of my father has caused me to neglect my studies

33 Being a CICL was regrettable experience

34 Inside MYRC that I discovered myself

35 My friends never cared to visit me or bothered to send food or medicine when I was sick

36 I realized that they were with me only in times of enjoyment

37 I also realized that there are people who are willing to help me

38 I learned that all of these have to start with me

39 Struggles when my father's death and h didn't find justice

40 I adore my family because they keep me pushing to enlighten me and motivate me to continue my life without my father

Co-Researcher 2

"A Love for Family without Hatred despite of Negligence"

"I am Aga. I firmly believe that success comes to those who work hard for it. I was born out of wedlock and my parents have their own respective families now. My maternal grandmother, Lola Miling, raised me all by herself. She told me that my parents were still teenagers when they lived together under one roof. My mother was only 15 years old, while my father was 17. Because of that, there were many things they argued about most of the time, which later led to their separation. I never knew who my father was; he left my mother before I was even born. My mother has a new live-in partner. According to Lola Miling, my stepfather did not want me to live with them. Lola Miling sells fruits and vegetables in the market near our house. She doesn't earn much, that's why I could not continue my studies after I graduated from elementary. But I always wanted to return to school. I wanted to finish my studies and become successful someday so that I may provide Lola Miling a comfortable life.

Before they admitted me to MYRC, I was a simple boy who dreamed of becoming successful one day. Before I sleep, I used to think that one day, I will have all the things I dreamed of–a fully furnished house and, of course, money to buy delicious food and all the other things that Lolang Miling and I need. Lola Miling is ageing; I wanted to give her a comfortable life one day. I think about these before I sleep. I am an average student, but a diligent one. I immediately go home from school so that I have ample time to do my homework, while my grandmother was busy with household chores.

I often asked my grandmother about my father's whereabouts. Her answer is the same–she does not know where my father is and that it would be futile to look for him. My mother seldom visits us. She said her new partner is strict and does not want her to visit us often, or even stay longer than an hour. My stepfather does not even bother accompanying my mother whenever she comes to visit. Sometimes, I see her giving Lola Miling some money for our daily expenses. I am thankful for her financial help; but I am longing for something more. I often asked myself if my parents ever loved me at all, or much less, wanted me. I could not remember a time when my mother hugged me when I was scared, or took care of me when I was sick. Sometimes I envy other children, because of the love and care they receive from their parents and other family members. I pity my grandmother because she is already old, and yet, instead of enjoying her remaining years, she has to work hard for the two of us. She has to get up really early each day to sell fruits and vegetables, because if she doesn't, we would starve.

One day, Lola Miling got sick. I did not go to school so I could take care of her. The sad part was that she could not sell her fruits and vegetables, thus, we barely had anything to eat because she was sick for several days. I had to plead with the owner of a nearby sari-sari store for some instant noodles and cans of sardines. I told her we would pay her as soon as my grandmother gets better. One day, while I was begging the sari-sari store owner to lend me some food, a stranger came to me and asked what the problem was. I narrated him my story. Much to my utter surprise, he took out his wallet and gave some cash to the sari-sari store owner. Not only did he pay for our debt, but he even told the sari-sari store owner to give me everything I needed and he will pay for it. I thanked the kind man and thought that he must have taken pity on me. After the sari-sari store owner gave me everything I needed, I rushed back to our house to prepare our lunch.

After several days, while I was walking on the street, I saw the kind man again and he inquired about my grandmother. I told him that my grandmother was already better, and she has resumed selling fruits and vegetables in the market. I thanked him again for the generosity he showed us. He said it was nothing. He asked me about my age. When I told him I was already 15, he asked me if I wanted to earn some money. I immediately replied, I wanted to earn extra money to help my grandmother. He told me to go out of the house later that night to meet him at the sari-sari store where we first met and he will give the details then. He told me never to tell anyone, not even my grandmother, that we talked and that we were planning to meet later that night because my grandmother might not allow me.

That night, my grandmother went to sleep early. As soon as she closed her eyes, I slowly crept towards the door and gently unhinged the lock. I scurried towards the sari-sari store; but before I even got there, I already saw the man patiently waiting for me, with a cigarette between his lips. I greeted the kind man, and he instructed me to get inside a parked tricycle. While inside, he told me what I was supposed to do. He said my only job would be to squeeze myself inside one window and open the door once I get in the house. He told me it was a simple job, considering that I am small and thin for my age. He also convinced me that no harm would come to me because that is a menial task compared to what they will do. He will give me money after doing what they ask me to do. Though apprehensive, I obeyed his order because I badly needed the money. I thought, with the money I'll be earning, I may return to school to finish my studies, and I will also help my grandmother with the daily expenses.

Because I was thin and small, I did not have a hard time squeezing myself inside an open window, and immediately upon entry, I opened the door so that the man and the tricycle driver can come in. The man told me to wait inside the tricycle, which I did, and after half an hour later, they hurriedly boarded the tricycle and they brought a lot of stuff with them–cellphones, a laptop, a flat screen TV and a lot more expensive things. Before we returned to where I live, we stopped in a small house and they placed their loot there. When we arrived at my destination, the man handed me a five hundred peso bill. I was happy because it was my first time to see and have that much money. I hurriedly went inside our house and it was fortunate that Lola Miling was still sleeping soundly. The next day, I tried to wake up at the same time my grandmother did so that she won't suspect anything, but as soon as she left for the market, I slept again and woke up only when I felt hungry. I remembered I had five hundred pesos, and I felt excited because for the first time, I'll be able to eat anything I want. I went to the nearest fast food and looked at the menu above the counter.

I wanted to order everything that was on the menu, because I also wanted to give some food to my grandmother, but I knew she would be suspicious, hence I ordered enough food for myself and I returned home. While I was walking home, I looked sideways on the street, hoping to find the man I was with yesterday. I thought to myself, if I ever saw him again and asked me to go with him, I would not hesitate. I know that what I did was wrong, but I promise to stop once I had enough savings to resume my studies. I was about to turn a corner when a figure blocked my way. When I looked up, I saw him again. He told me we have work later that night, and just like last night, he will wait for me at the sari-sari store. Before we parted ways, he handed me a cellphone and told me he would call me up later. I nodded and quickly walked towards our house for fear that someone might see me talking to the man. I know nothing about him, not even his name, and because I was in such a hurry, I could not ask his name.

When I arrived home, I immediately opened the food I ordered: 2-piece chicken with extra rice, ice cream and a large fry. I had a sumptuous meal; I was so full. I almost could not stand. After eating, I tidied up and threw the trash outside our house so as not to raise suspicion from my grandmother. Before Lola Miling arrived, I already cooked rice and bought canned meat loaf in the sari-sari store. The store's owner was surprised when I handed my payment for the canned meat loaf, but she said nothing. Lola Miling was equally surprised when she arrived because I was already setting the table. She asked me where I got the money to buy our viand. I told her I helped an elderly woman carry her groceries, and I was paid enough to buy viand.

I did not mean to lie to my grandmother, but I was certain she would get mad and scold me if she found out the truth.

After we ate, I tidied the table while Lola Miling washed the dishes. After cleaning the table, I secretly looked at the cellphone which the man gave me, and there I saw he has a message for me. I did not know how to use a cellphone, but since it was a basic phone, it was easy for me to use it. After reading the message, I simply replied "ok." I arrived at the sari-sari store at exactly 9:00 p.m. because I did not wait for my grandmother to fall asleep. I stepped out of our house as soon as she turned her back on the door. The man was not there yet when I arrived. I looked at the cellphone and checked his message once more. I was right; the message said 9:00 p.m. A few minutes later, a tricycle stopped in front of me. After recognizing the tricycle driver, I boarded. While in transit to our destination, I asked the man's name. He said he is Mando. I wanted to ask so many questions but opted not to because Mang Mando lighted a cigarette and smoked.

After some time, the tricycle stopped, meaning we arrived at our destination. The tricycle driver signaled for me to do my job, thus I got off the tricycle. This time, it was already easy for me to get inside the house because the main gate was not locked, and the window was huge enough. I did not have to squeeze myself in. I opened the door to let Mang Mando and the tricycle driver in. Instead of waiting inside the tricycle, I helped them stole stuff inside the house. There were more valuable things in this house than the previous one, because we could steal an assortment of gadgets and jewelries. There were even expensive pairs of shoes and small appliances. Mang Mando must have done excellent surveillance on these houses. No one was inside the house when we arrived. I left the main gates unlocked and there was lots of valuable stuff.

After we delivered the stolen stuff, the driver drove to my place and before I got off the tricycle, Mang Mando handed me a couple of one thousand peso bills. He said it was my bonus for helping them. He also told me I can rest for a couple of nights because we have to lie low for now. He said he would text me if he needed me. He instructed me to buy a charger so I can charge my cellphone. The next day, after Lola Miling left for the market, I changed clothes and headed outside to buy my food and charger for my cellphone. I have more money now, thus I have to be more careful so that Lola Miling will suspect nothing. After I returned home, I immediately charged my phone while I ate. A week after, I received another text message from

Mang Mando instructing me to meet him at exactly 9:00 p.m. at the sari-sari store. It was fortunate that Lolang Miling immediately fell asleep; the moment she closed her eyes, I rushed to the door and gently closed it as I walked towards the street.

I had been standing for a couple of minutes when the tricycle pulled over. I boarded inside and the tricycle sped off. Mang Mando said that our destination's farther than the first two, but he assured me that there is more stuff there, much more than the two houses combined. I was thinking about where we were headed. I was worried because my grandmother might catch me if I come home too late. An hour later, we stopped in front of a very large, dark house. Before I got off the tricycle, Mang Mando told me I will do it on my own this time, a test of sorts, he said. Though hesitant, I obeyed him because I have not saved enough money to resume my studies. I opened the gate and squeezed my way through a small window, and when I entered, I put every valuable thing I can find inside the gigantic bag Mang Mando gave me. I even pocketed some cash and jewelries I found inside a drawer, for myself, in case I did not get paid enough later. When I thought I had scraped the entire house of every valuable item I could find, I opened the door so I could go out, but I was surprised to see several cops outside the house. Mang Mando and the tricycle driver were nowhere to be found.

One cop handcuffed me. He was saying stuff I could not understand, perhaps because I only finished elementary, or because I was so confused. I did not really know what was going on. I wanted to ask the cop where I actually am, and where my companions were, because I thought I should not be the only one apprehended by the cops. When we arrived at the police station, one cop asked for my details. After answering all the questions, I asked what will happen to me. She replied I will be brought to MYRC, a facility for children in conflict with the law. I told her I did not do it by myself. I told her I had two male companions inside the tricycle; and the mastermind instructed me to go inside the house by myself, and they would just wait for me inside the tricycle. She said there was no tricycle in sight when they arrived. I felt betrayed. Instantly, I also felt remorseful. I know there was nothing I can do now, so I just pleaded with the cop to contact my grandmother and inform her of my present situation.

When I arrived in MYRC, the staff-members were surprised because they could not believe I was already 15 years old. The social worker who would handle my case oriented me towards the rules and regulations of the institution. She also told me the corresponding sanction for every violation. Also, she interviewed me and asked the same questions that the cop asked when I was at the police station. Somehow, I felt I had more freedom to ask my social worker anything concerning my case. Her manner of speaking was far gentler than the cop who was interviewing me in the police station. I told the social worker everything; how I was single-handedly raised by Lola Miling, and how impoverished our life was, the very reason I was drawn to stealing stuff from inside other people's houses.

As I recounted my story, I was close to tears because I knew how much I disappointed my grandmother. I requested my social worker to inform my grandmother of my current situation because I knew she must be worried sick by then. The social worker said she will do her best to inform my grandmother that I was in MYRC. After several weeks, Lola Miling finally visited me. She was crying profusely while the social worker explained she had a hard time locating Lola Miling. She then allowed Lola Miling and I to talk for some time. Lola Miling told me that the social worker already explained everything to her, even the options we may take for my best interest and welfare. I was so ashamed of what I did and I was also crying as I asked for forgiveness from my grandmother. I told her I will do my best to behave while inside the center.

I wish for the government to pay more attention to institutions like MYRC. It has been built a long time ago, and the dormitories are no longer fit for the number of wards that are continuously increasing. Further, the facilities of MYRC are not enough for CICLs, even the staff are not enough. There were days when my social worker did not talk to me because she had other clients that she had to interview. She explained that as much as she could; she allots equal amount of time to all her clients, as well as attend to other matters such as home visits, court hearings and paper works. I wish that the government would realize the importance of institutions like MYRC for the holistic reform of CICLs like me. I also wish that more institutions like MYRC will be built to facilitate the increasing number of CICLs.

Life inside MYRC was difficult. I was used to an impoverished life, but I found it difficult to adjust to the center. There were nights when I cried to sleep because of what happened to me. I promised myself that I will do my best not to violate any rules or regulations inside the center. Aside from that, I also promised myself that I would not wait until they release me from the center to plan a better future for myself, and for Lola Miling. I enrolled in the Alternative Learning System (ALS) inside MYRC and, according to my social worker, my teacher has positive feedback. The teacher said that I was an industrious student; that I diligently did my homework, and I always came to class neat and prepared. She said, I can easily understand the lesson, and that she did not have a hard explaining each lesson to me, so much so that she assigned me as tutor to my dorm mates who could not catch up to the lessons. This experience has taught me that anything gained from any wrongdoing will not result from something good, and that change, though hard and slow, can always happen even while I am still inside the center. I have here a circle, a very simple circle, but so many things inside of it; inside of this circle is my family. I'm not so good in Arts so I will explain it to the best of my ability. My father and my mother and my grandmother are inside of my circle; all of them are important to me. They play a vital role in my life. Sad to say, their roles are not good somehow in my growing life. I'm a product of broken family. My mother and father, in their early age, lived together; however, because they were young, they failed to raise me properly. They separated and left me to my grandmother. It was my grandmother who stood by my side and tried her best to provide everything to me.

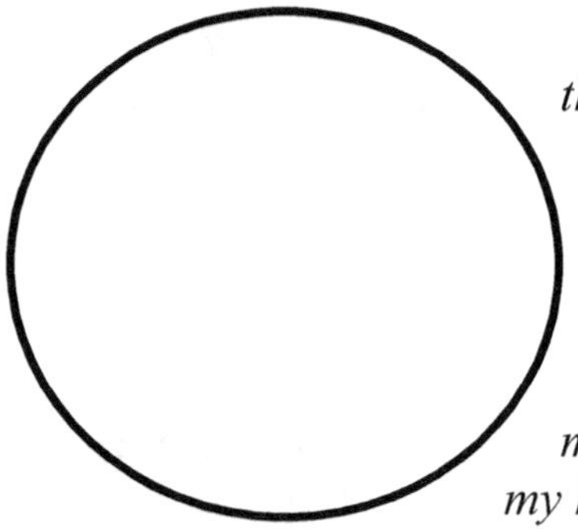

Figure 8: Circle Symbol

The circle that I draw means I wanted to put my family in it and all the people who are important to me. I wanted to keep them, be with them. Even if we have terrible memories to share with, I still want to keep them. The thing is, I love them; they are my family. Inside this institution, there's no other person who cares for me, who looks after me and who loves me the most. Only my family believed in me and shares my struggle in life. Yes, I have regrets about my father and mother, but it makes little sense to keep my hatred towards them inside my heart. I still owe to them who I am and why I exist in this world. I want to keep my family as much as I can because family is love and forever I will be thankful to all of them."

First Reflection: Textual Themes

1. I firmly believe that success comes to those who works hard for it
2. I was born out of wedlock and my parents have their own families now
3. My maternal grandmother, Lola Miling, raised me all by herself
4. I never knew who my father was, he already left my mother before I was even born
5. Lola Miling doesn't earn much, that's why I was not able to continue my studies after I graduated from elementary
6. I wanted to finish my studies and become successful someday so that I may provide grandma a comfortable life
7. I was a simple boy who dreamed of becoming successful one day
8. Lola Miling is already ageing and I wanted to give her a comfortable life one day
9. I was thankful to the financial help of my mother but I was longing for something more
10. I often asked myself if my parents ever loved me at all
11. I envied other children, because of the love and care they receive from their parents and other family members
12. Lola Miling had to work hard for the two of us so that we will not starve
13. We barely had anything to eat because she was sick for several days
14. A stranger man helped me to pay our debt in the sari-sari store
15. I obey his order because I badly needed money
16. I was happy because t was my first time to see and have that much money
17. I know that what I did was wrong but I promise to stop once I had enough savings to resume my studies
18. I did not mean to lie to my grandmother, but I am certain she will get mad and scold me if she found out the truth
19. I helped them stole stuff inside the house
20. There is more stuff there, much more than the two houses combined
21. I was a bit worried because my grandmother might catch me if I came home too late
22. Though hesitant, I obeyed him because I have not saved enough money to resume my studies
23. I could not understand, perhaps because I only finished elementary, or because I was so confused
24. I felt betrayed and instantly I also felt remorseful
25. I know there was nothing I can do now
26. I felt that I have more freedom to ask my social worker anything concerning my case
27. I was close to tears because I knew how much I disappointed my grandmother
28. I was so ashamed of what I did and I was also crying as I asked for forgiveness from my grandmother
29. I told her that I will do my best to behave while inside the center
30. The facilities and staff of MYRC are not enough for CICL
31. More institution like MYR will be built to facilitate the increasing number of CICL
32. Life inside MYC was not easy, I was used to an impoverished life but I found it difficult to adjust inside the center
33. I promised myself that I will do my best not to violate any rules or regulations inside the center

Co-Researcher 3

"Enviousness Leads To Agony and Desperation"

My name is Jaja, seventeen years old. I am the youngest among five children. I am the only one studying. My parents have a stall in Divisoria where they sell fruits, vegetables, food seasoning and other items related to food. My older siblings have all graduated from college and are now employed. My parents did not have to work anymore; but because they wanted me to study in a private school, and because they did not want to force my older siblings to pay for my tuition fee and other expenses, they continued to work hard and strive each day so that they could fulfill their desire of sending me to a private university. I could honestly say that I am luckier compared to my classmates in high school. My weekly allowance was more than enough for my daily expenses; hence I get the chance to spend time in malls with my classmates. Sometimes, I ask permission from my parents so that I could drink beer with my classmates inside our house. My parents are okay with that because they said I am old enough and since I am a teenage boy, it is natural for me to drink. My older siblings, however, are not so keen on the idea, thus they often advise me not to drink too much, or not to spend too much time at the mall during weekends. They also told me to study hard so as not to disappoint our parents.

Most of the time, if I needed anything or wanted anything, I just had to ask my older siblings and they give to me because they are all gainfully employed and all are still single. They also share in household expenses. That's why I can say that whatever amount my parents earn, they save it for my future enrollment in college, and for other emergency expenses.

When I finally enrolled in a private university, I surprised to know that my classmates were far richer than I am. They have the latest cellphones; they wear branded outfits from head to foot; even their hankies and face towels were all branded. Back in high school, I was used to being the only student with nice clothes, nice cellphone and extra money. But in college, it was completely different. Suddenly, my self-perception changed. I began comparing myself to my college classmates. Some of them even have their own cars while I commute to and from the university. One night, while we were having dinner, I casually asked my parents if they could at least buy me a motorcycle, so I would not have a hard time travelling to and from the university. I also told them that owning a motorcycle would be convenient for me because I could put a lot of things inside the compartment box and would not have to worry about forgetting P.E. uniforms, projects or assignments left at home. I did not expect that they would actually buy me a brand new motorcycle. I thought, maybe, if I asked them for a car instead, they could still afford it, given their high daily income from their stall. I thought that maybe, after a few months, I will ask them for a new car.

My father strictly told me never to drink and drive, which I obeyed. I did not want to disappoint my parents and, of course; I did not want to be involved in a motorcycle accident. When I went to school on board my new motorcycle, my classmates were in awe. They probably did not think my parents could afford to buy me a brand new motorcycle. I became instantly famous. Some of my classmates, those who did not talk to me before, became friendly to me suddenly. Others invited me for a "joy ride," which I cordially declined because I promised my parents that I will only use my motorcycle to get to and from the school in a short amount of time. A month passed. As I was parking outside the school, I saw a handful of students huddled around someone or something, which blocked from my view. When I walked towards them, I saw one of my classmates with his brand new car. He said it was a gift from his parents. I can't help but feel envious. I thought, how am I going to compete with that? Is this what college life is all about? If a student has the latest car or phone model, he or she is famous, until another student comes to school with a flashier car or more expensive gadget.

I was contemplating on the idea of asking my parents for a new car, but I know they would disagree and scold me instead because my motorcycle is still fairly new. I could not sit still all day, I was thinking about my classmate's new car. I could not get it off my head and even if I tell myself that my parents would not buy me a car even if they could afford it, I still can't shake it off my head. My parents have been working so hard for me, to send me to a private university and give me a weekly allowance that is more than enough, but I was consumed by an unbearable envy that I talked about it even as we dined that evening at home. As I was talking to them about how my classmate was gifted with a brand new car by his parents, and how the car was so beautiful and flashy, my father had already guessed what I was going to say next. He told me that no, they could not afford to buy me a new car, and that it would be too much if I would insist on getting a new car. He further said that I might lose focus on my studies and just drive around the city or anywhere I want to go if they heeded my desire. I silently finished my supper and headed to my bedroom afterwards. A couple of minutes later, I heard a soft knock on my door. When I opened it, my oldest sister came in. She told me; she knew how I felt. She knew college life was hard. It was unlike in elementary or high school where everybody knew everyone else and where every student is almost equal in terms of financial status. She also said that even she had a hard time, even if she was studying as a scholar in a prestigious semi-private university because some of her classmates are rich. She knew how envious I was with my classmate and his new, flashy car but she said, instead of being envious, I should use it as an inspiration to study harder, to become successful in my chosen profession. I thanked her for the advice and told her I have to sleep because I had to be up early.

The next day, I absented myself from school; I told my parents that I was not feeling well, and that I'd rather stay at home to rest. Truth is, I felt bad because I did not get what I wanted this time, and they did not use me for that. I knew that if only they combined all of their money, they could afford to buy me a car, but they did not. I know I was being irrational and selfish, but since my envy still consumed me, I did not accept any reasonable explanation or justification for not getting what I wanted. I thought they were depriving me of what I wanted. I was asleep all day, and had to eat what was left on the table, a few pieces of hot dog, an egg and stale fried rice. I did not bother cooking because I did not have the appetite, plus I did not how to cook, anyway. Even during supper, I did not join my family because I thought if I did not talk to all of them, they would change their mind and buy me a new car. Even before sleeping, I still think about how cool I would be if I have a new car, I could go to a lot places, I have bragging rights, and I would meet a lot of students from other courses.

When I woke up the next morning, I went to school, and much as I did not want it, I was the first to talk to my mother because I needed to ask for money from her. After handling me my allowance, I hurried outside without even saying goodbye. When I reached the school, I slowly walked towards our classroom. I felt lethargic, but I did not want to be absent anymore. As I walked inside the classroom, I saw one of my classmates, the one with a new and flashy car, counting a lot of money. We were both surprised upon seeing each other; I was surprised by how much money he was counting, while he was surprised that someone else had also gone to school early. His name was Rick, only child and orphaned by his mother at an early age. He said that his mother has a new family, and they were living in the United States, while he was presently living with his paternal aunt here in Manila. He also said that his father's job pays well, thus his father can afford to buy him everything he wanted. Once again, I felt a pang of envy, which did not escape Rick, and when he noticed I was envious, he stopped talking about his life.

As the days went by, Rick and I slowly became close. He no longer talked much about his life, but he often asked me to accompany him everywhere–playing billiards with some of our classmates in Intramuros, drinking beer with his friends in Tondo. Sometimes, Rick and I spent time in a secluded park near our school. I was hesitant the first time he invited because I did not know him that much; I thought I might get into trouble if I hang out with him, but he assured me that everything will be all right. So I went with him and we went to what Intramuros students called "walls." A handful of students were already there when we arrived–some were idling away while some were studying for an exam or a graded recitation.

Rick walked farther away from the students, and as I followed him, I wondered why he wanted to be as far away from other people as possible. After a couple of minutes, Rick stopped at a deserted spot and after ensuring that no one else was there besides us, he opened his backpack and told me he had something to show to me. He told me that no one else knows about this and that I must promise never to tell it to anyone else. When he opened his backpack, he showed me a huge, clear Ziploc bag containing what seemed to be like dried weeds or grass, and I immediately thought that Rick must have lost his mind to be showing me this. When Rick realized I did not know what he was showing me, he started laughing. He laughed so hard that I felt insulted. He asked me if I seriously did not know what he was showing me, and I replied, no, I seriously did not know what those dried leaves were.

He told me that those were dried marijuana leaves, and those were the reason he always had a lot of money, and the reason he was showing it to me was because he knew I became envious of his flashy car and money. Again, I felt insulted. I did not think I was too obvious, or that I was already wearing my heart on my sleeve. He patted my back and told me it was okay, and if I wanted to have lots of money like him, he was more than willing to make me his partner in selling marijuana. I did not think twice because I really wanted to buy a car someday, and not only that, I also wanted to buy more expensive stuff like clothes, gadgets and shoes that I can use in school. I also thought that if I was going to earn as much as Rick does, I could live independently, away from my controlling parents and nagging older siblings.

Rick taught me everything I needed to learn about selling marijuana.–he introduced me to prospective clients and told them they could now contact me if they needed a marijuana fix. He also took me to his "suppliers" and they welcomed me like I was a long-lost brother. They all said I could start with a couple of grams, because that was how they all started–small. After I gained my initial supply, Rick instructed me to observe him, which I did. All of his transactions went smoothly. He was so used to it; it was like second nature to him. After several days of observation, it was my turn to sell marijuana, but I had a hard time doing it. Perhaps I was too nervous, especially since I had to do it on school premises. I always thought that I might get caught in the act of actually selling marijuana by one of the roving security guards. I did not know that Rick was observing me while I was doing it. After I finished my last transaction, Rick talked to me. I thought he was going to tell me to stop selling because we both might get caught since I was obviously nervous; instead, he told me that from now on, he will tell his contacts in our school that I will be the one supplying them marijuana. We carefully planned our moves so we won't get caught by the school's security guards.

We executed our plan very well and before I knew it, I sold more than I could imagine. I never thought I could have this much money in such a short time, and most of my money was safely and secretly tucked away inside my room. Because Rick and I were so engrossed with what we were doing, we did not realize that it was almost the end of another semester. I still attended all of my classes because Rick and I even planned about the days we're going to absent ourselves from our classes. The only setback was I slowly veered myself away from my family and my other classmates. Sometimes I got home in the wee hours of the morning, but left very early for school the next day.

Before the semester ended, Rick discussed to me he still has a bag full of marijuana which he planned to sell before the semestral break. He invited me to go to the "walls" after our last exam to sell the remaining marijuana. I told him it might not be a good idea to sell marijuana in such an open space, even if it was almost deserted. He said he will take care of everything so I did not have to worry about a thing. All I had to do, he said, was show up in the agreed place after our last exam. So off to the "walls," I went after my last exam. While I was walking towards the "walls," I was again nervous. I tried to shake it off because I thought I needed the money and I did not want to disappoint Rick. When I arrived, Rick was already there, along with some students who wanted a marijuana fix. We were busy joking around and selling marijuana that we failed to notice 3 cops walking towards us.

Things happened so quickly. The cops immediately handcuffed Rick and me while the other students scrambled in all directions, away from the cops. When we arrived at the police station, I pleaded with one cop to allow me to call my mother using my cellphone, and she agreed. After I talked to my mother, I asked the cop where Rick was. She told me that Rick was already inside a prison cell for adult offenders. It was only then that I discovered Rick was no longer a minor. His father was not really rich. When my mother came to the police station, I thought she came by herself, but I was ashamed because my father and my older siblings were also with her. The cop explained to them I will be transferred to MYRC after the inquest procedure.

I arrived in MYRC accompanied by my parents and my oldest sister. She said that she had to accompany my parents to assist my mother in case her blood pressure rises. I did not know my mother had a heart ailment, and that she almost had a heart attack when she learned of my situation. The social worker explained the rules and regulations of the institution, as well as the sanctions to each violation. My mother asked if they could bring me food three times a week. The social worker declined because she made us understand the importance of following the rules and regulations of the center. She also said that it is imperative that I learn to adapt to my new environment.

I could not sleep at all during my first few nights in MYRC. I had a tough time adjusting to life inside the institution; I missed my bedroom; I missed using my cellphone and laptop; I missed my mother's cooking. Most especially, I missed my family. My parents saw how quickly I lost weight. So what they did was to bring lots of food each time they visited me at MYRC. The food they brought was not just for me, but also for my dorm mates. I knew it was a burden for my parents, physically and financially.

It was only now that I realize how much they have sacrificed for me. I was so remorseful for what I did because despite all the disappointments I gave them; they continued to support me, and they never abandoned me. The social worker gave me the same support my parents did, and for that, I am forever grateful. Sometimes I broke a rule or two, but my social worker had been considerate of me. She also made me understand the importance of doing my best to get along with the other CICLs in the center, and to show respect to all the staff at all times.

To the government, I wish that they also give importance to us CICLs. Being a CICL does not define us; we can correct our mistakes and we can change for the better. I had dorm mates who were "marked" by cops just because they had been admitted to MYRC once. I wish this stigma would end so that we can be fully rehabilitated and prove we can also be productive members of the society.

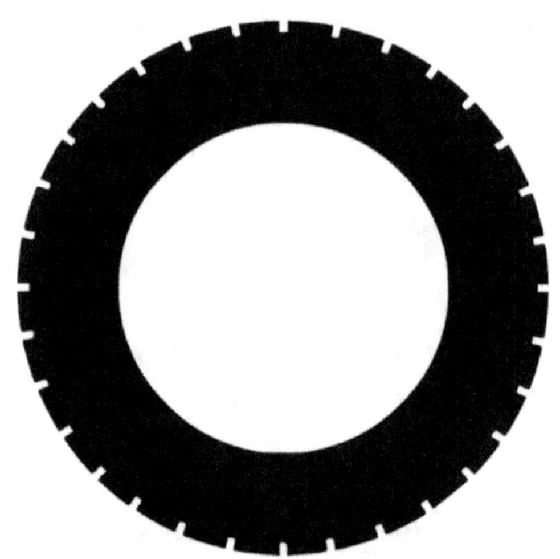

Figure 9: Circle Symbol

Being a CICL has taught me that nothing good can come out of envy. At night before I sleep, I think about all the things that happened to me. I realized that had I been content with what my parents worked so hard to give me, had I not coveted the things that Rick possessed, I would not be in this situation now. Here at MYRC, I learned to adapt to my surroundings, to get along with all kinds of people. I also learned a very important lesson: that not everything I wanted will be handed to me on a silver platter and that I will not always be prioritized. I became appreciative of the things I have now, and I am grateful for the people who continue to support me during my hardest times. Being in MYRC taught me to have stronger faith in GOD; I learned to offer everything to HIM, all my fears, doubts and minor triumphs each day. I learned to pray for forgiveness for all my sins, and to pray for salvation, not only of myself, but of my family as well. My drawing represents my entire experience inside MYRC and my thoughts. I drew a circle because prior to my confinement in MYRC, my life was easy. My family provided everything I needed I'm the youngest among my four siblings. Both my parents are hard worker. They augment a living by selling fruits and vegetables. Considering all of my siblings are working I can ask money easily from them for my allowance. Drawing a circle means all I thought was my easy life will not end and it will just move around and around. Because of that thought, I truly enjoyed the privilege of being the youngest.

I was in senior high school when I was caught selling illegal drugs. Hence, I can connect my "circle" drawing to a simple life to a "hard life" inside MYRC. A circle has two meanings. First is my simple life; and then, second, is my darkest life.

I consider my first month in MYRC as an endless agony and in my life. I thought that just like a circle; it seemed endless and will not stop just like the circle that has no end. I cannot complain; I cannot stop blaming myself because I'm the one who put myself in this circle of pain, agony, and desperation. I feel I am not trustworthy of anything. My family still showed concern in my trying times and gave me a second chance, which I don't deserve somehow. At present, I am proving my worth to my family. I am keeping my right back. This is my priority. This is my circle of positive life; it empowers me as always to strive harder.

First Reflection: Textual Themes

1. I am the youngest among five children, and I am the only one studying.
2. My parents have a stall in Divisoria where they sell fruits, vegetables, food seasoning and other items related to food.
3. My older siblings have all graduated from college and are now gainfully employed
4. My parents continued to work hard and strive each day so that they could fulfill their desire of sending me to a private university.
5. My parents are okay with me if I drink because they said I am old enough and since I am a teenage boy, it is natural for me to drink at times; my older siblings, however, are not so keen on the idea thus they often advise me not to drink too much
6. They also told me to study hard so as not to disappoint our parents.
7. I just had to ask my older siblings and they give it to me because they are all gainfully employed and all are still single.
8. Enrolled in a private university, I was surprised because my classmates were far richer than I am; I began comparing myself to my college classmates;
9. I did not expect that they would actually buy me a brand new motorcycle
10. I did not want to disappoint my parents and of course I became famous; some of my classmates, those who did not talk to me before, became friendly to me all of a sudden. I can't help but feel envious
11. My parents have been working so hard for me to send me to a private university; they gave me a weekly allowance that is more than enough
12. I was consumed by an unbearable envy with the flashy car of my classmate that I talked about it to my family as we dined that evening at home. My parents were opposed to buying a car saying I might lose focus on my studies and just drive around the city or anywhere I want to go if they heeded my desire.
13. My older sister told me, she knew how I felt; she knew college life was hard. Instead of being envious, I should use it as an inspiration to study harder
14. I felt bad because I did not get what I wanted this time, and I was not used to it. I know I was being irrational and selfish, but since my envy still consumed me, I did not accept any reasonable explanation or justification for not getting what I wanted.
15. I felt lethargic but I did not want to be absent anymore; I felt a pang of envy, which did not escape Rick, and when he noticed I was envious, he stopped talking about his life.

16. I was hesitant the first time he invited me because I did not know him that much. I thought that I might get into trouble if I hang out with him, but he assured me that everything will be all right.

17. He told me that those were dried marijuana leaves and those were the reason he always had a lot of money. I felt insulted; I did not think I was too obvious, or that I was already wearing my heart on my sleeve

18. I wanted to have lots of money like him; he was more than willing to make me his partner in selling marijuana. I did not think twice because I really wanted to buy a car someday, and not only that, I also wanted to buy more expensive stuff like clothes, gadgets and shoes that I can use in school.

19. I could live independently, away from my controlling parents and nagging older siblings.

20. I was too nervous, especially since I had to do it inside school premises; I always thought that I might get caught on the act of actually selling marijuana by one of the roving security guards

21. We were able to execute our plan very well and before I knew it, I sold more than I could imagine; Rick and I were so engrossed with what we were doing

22. The only setback was I slowly veered myself away from my family and my other classmates; I tried to shake it off because I thought, I needed the money and I did not want to disappoint Rick.

23. Things happened so quickly; the cops immediately handcuffed Rick and me. I discovered that Rick was no longer a minor, and that his father is not really rich

24. I was ashamed because my father and my older siblings were also with her. I did not know my mother had a heart ailment, and that she almost had a heart attack when she learned of my situation.

25. I was not able to sleep at all during my first few nights in MYRC. I had a tough time adjusting to life inside the institution, I miss my family

26. I know it was a burden for my parents, physically and financially, and it was only now that I realize how much they have sacrificed for me

27. I was so remorseful for what I did because despite all the disappointment I gave them, they continued to support me, and they never abandoned me.

28. The social worker gave me the same support my parents give, and for that I am forever grateful. She also made me understand the importance of doing my best to get along with the other CICLs in the center

29. She also made me understand the importance of doing my best to get along with the other CICLs in the center give importance to us CICLs that being a CICL does not define us, and that we are capable of correcting our mistakes and that we have the capacity to change for the better.

30. As soon as stigma ends and we can be fully rehabilitated, we will have the opportunity to prove that we can also be productive members of the society.

31. Being a CICL has taught me that nothing good can come out from being envious, I realized, had I been content with what my parents worked so hard to give me
32. I learned to adapt to my surroundings, to get along with all kinds of people.
33. I also learned a very important lesson: that not everything I wanted will be handed to me on a silver platter, that I will not always be prioritized.
34. I became appreciative of the things I have now and I am grateful for the people who continued to support me during my hardest times.
35. Most importantly, being in MYRC taught me to have stronger faith in GOD; I learned to offer everything to HIM, all my fears, doubts and small triumphs each day.
36. I learned to pray, for forgiveness for all my sins, and to pray for salvation, not only of myself, but of my family as well; my family provides everything that I need.

37. My parents are hard worker; they augmented a living thru selling fruits and vegetables and considering that all of my siblings are working I can ask easily money for my allowances.
38. I can consider it as an endless agony and pain in my life. I can't complain; at the same time, I can't stop blaming myself because I'm the one who put myself in this circle of pain, agony, desperation that made me not trustworthy of anything.
39. My family still supported me in my trying times and gave me the second chance that I don't actually deserve.
40. Up to the present, I am proving my worth to my family and keeping my right track as my priority, and this circle of positive life empower me as always to strive harder.

Co-Researcher 4

"Standing Still Through Violence in Achieving Justice and Protection"

My name is Jashtin. I'm 17 years old. I am the eldest among a brood of 4. My parents separated when I was 7 years old. They use to always fight; my father abused my mother physically. I used to cry very hard until I fell asleep. I knew my father left our home, which made me more relieved because he abused me physically. When he was a stevedore, we always had financial problem. He was an alcoholic; every time he was mad, he will hurt us and express his regret with me being born and being married to my mother. As a young boy, I just cry and sleep in the arms of my mother.

When my father left us, my mother did everything she could to raise us. She worked as a laundry woman in the neighborhood. Sometimes, the only food served was a pack of noodles and a piece of fish for all siblings. She told me she will find a job the next day and will come home early for our food. I finished my breakfast and read my old books while taking care of my siblings. I was curious why my mother got food that was too much from our normal meals.

I was worried one time why my mother was still not home late at night. Our neighbor, Aling Yolly, gave some food for our dinner. It was ginisang sayote. We rarely eat this kind of food because we used to eat noodles, bread or fish only. After dinner, I let my siblings sleep. I told them I will wait for our mother. I fell asleep, yet she was not yet home. When I woke up the next day, my mother was still not at home. I was about to go to Aling Yolly to borrow some food when my mother entered the house with a plastic full of bread. She said that she just got home and lacking sleep. While we were eating, she asked me about our day yesterday without her. I told her everything was good; we were provided food by Aling Yolly. My mother has now a job at night. I asked her why the work was night time only. She did not answer me; instead she asked me to clean the table and take care of my siblings while she sleeps. She told me not to disturb her. She left money for our lunch and asked me to pay for our food last night at Aling Yolly.

Time went by fast. I was 14 years old when i learned to do household chores. I was also the one brought and picked up my siblings to schools. Now, I cannot teach myself to read and write because of my responsibilities at home. Sometimes, when my siblings are doing homework, I joined them. I asked questions about what it is to be in school. I felt envy.

My mother still works at nights. I have a little knowledge of her job while talking with Aling Yolly, but was still afraid to ask her. Sometimes she did not come home; but she made sure that we have food. One time, she told me she will be gone for 1 week. She gave me 1,000 pesos for our daily needs. She also gave some money to Aling Yolly to cook for us delicious and healthy food. I asked her where she will go, but she did not answer; she just went.

I thought I was used to being the only one taking care of the house, but I was wrong. It is hard to do all the responsibilities on my own, especially since I was only a 14-year-old boy. There were nights when I cannot stop my tears, not just because of tiredness, but also because of my mother's absence. I always pray for us to have a comfortable life. I still wanted to study. I wanted us to eat delicious food, to have nice clothes and for my mother to stop the job she was doing, and just take care of us. I know the Lord will make my prayers and dreams come true.

When we were eating our lunch, my mother entered the house with happiness in her eyes. She came back exactly one week after. It shocked me when I saw a man behind her. She wanted us to call him Tito Fausto. My mother told us that Tito Fausto is her husband. We are going to live with him in his house. We immediately pack our things, leave the house and travelled to our new home. Tito Fausto's house is way bigger than ours. It has 2 concrete floors. My mother brought us to our room and let my siblings rest after a long ride. I helped her cook our dinner. After dinner, I asked my mother if she won't go to work. Tito Fausto answered she will not work anymore and will just stay in the house and take care of us. I was glad and thanked God for making my prayers come true. I am now 15, and enrolled in Alternative Learning System.

Tito Fausto is a silent type of guy. He always goes to work early and comes home late. According to my mother, he is an employee of a private company. I have a lot of curious questions for them, but I was quiet. I can see that my mother is happy with Tito Fausto, and I'm happy for her. I am also happy that I am now studying. That is why I always obey my mother and we give our respect to Tito Fausto. I thought that we already have a comfortable life, but I was wrong.

After 2 years of living with Tito Fausto, I have known him very well. He was just like my father. I often saw my mother with bruises. I know that my mother endures pain because she does not want to go back to our previous life, where we did not go to school, where she would have to go back to her past job. Because of this situation, I told my siblings not to go downstairs if they are not yet called to eat. I cannot protect my mother from Tito Fausto, but I will do my best to protect my siblings against him.

When we were having dinner, my youngest sibling unintentionally pushed the glass full of water towards Tito Fausto. He suddenly grabbed my sibling and punched him uncontrollably. My mother and my other siblings cried and told Tito Fausto to stop; but he continued. I told my siblings to go upstairs while I went to the kitchen, where I can still hear my youngest sibling's loud cries. When I saw my youngest sibling's blood all over his face, I stabbed with a knife that I got in the kitchen. I didn't know how many times I did it. I will not forgive him for hurting my youngest sibling. Later on, the police officers and barangay officials responded and brought me to the police station. I knew there that I stabbed Tito Fausto five times, which led him to death.

I could not talk to my mother because they brought me to the Manila Youth Reception Centre (MYRC) the next day. A social worker came to me and said that he will try his best to help me. When I entered the dorm, they gave me food and a place to sleep. Days passed, my mother did not visit me. I know she was taking care of my siblings or she did not know where I was.

My social worker told me that my mother knew I was in MYRC. She just cannot visit me because of my younger siblings. My youngest sibling whom Tito Fausto injured is now in good condition. They came back to our house before, which made me sad. But when I thought of what happened, the anger comes back.

I am used to living a hard life; it became easy for me to stay inside the MYRC. I am always picking a fight with my co-wards because of a little misunderstanding. I am an obedient child, especially for rules and regulation of the MYRC, but I do not approve a bully towards weak and vulnerable children.

I thanked my social worker for always reminding me to be calm at all times to prevent a fight against other children. I hope the government could provide enough help to the family of a CICL like me. When I was outside, I was always with my siblings; I looked after them. Now, I am worried about them, especially when my mother is at work. I hope that the government will have Skills Training Programs for us when we are released from the MYRC. I want to gain knowledge to help my family.

Figure 10: Tree Symbol

During my stay in the MYRC, I realized that anger will never be good in my life. I regret what I did and continuously pray to God that my family will still accept me.

My drawing is a tree. My entire life is full of battle, hardships in life; but I'm still standing and keep pushing to achieve my goals in life. I came from a broken family, eldest to my 3 siblings and now enjoying my freedom, which is the most important. My tree drawing is just like me, who stands all kinds of weather and still keeps standing. I can also compare my tree drawing to my mother, who stands as solo parent. Just like a tree who bears fruits and takes care of it on her own, a tree is also my family, who stands and stays with our mother no matter how difficult life could it be.

This life is challenging and full of hatred. If you choose to give up and let other people win, surely you will not be successful in life. A tree stands her ground and only bends when a strong wind, typhoon, tries to sneak and challenge her agility. I like how a tree blends and adjusts in times of challenges. I need to do the same thing for me to overcome all challenges in life."

First Reflection: Textual Themes

1 My parents separated when i was 7 years old.

2 They were always fighting to the point that my father began to abuse my mother physically.

3 I was also physically abused by him.

4 He was an alcoholic and every time he is mad, he will hurt us and express his regret

5 I just cried and sleep in the arms of my mother.

6 When my father left us, my mother did everything she could to raise us.

7 My mother told me that she cannot support my studies anymore; I was forced to educate myself while taking care of my younger siblings.

8 I started to read my old books while taking care of my siblings.

9 Our neighbor, Aling Yolly, gave some food for our dinner.

10 My mother has now a job at night.

11 I was the one who brought and picked up my siblings to and from the school.

12 I was not able to teach myself to read and write because of my responsibilities at home

13 I joined them and asked questions of what it was being in school which made me feel envious.

14 I have little knowledge about her job while talking with Aling Yolly but Iwas still afraid to ask her;

15 She did not come home but she made sure that we have food.

16 It is hard to do all the responsibilities on my own, especially I am only a 14 year old boy.

17 There were nights I could not stop my tears, not just because of tiredness, but also because of my mother's absence.

18 I always prayed for us to have a comfortable life

19 I still wanted to study

20 I wanted mother to stop her job and just take care of us.

21 I know that the Lord will make my prayers and dreams come.

22 Tito Fausto answered she (my mother) will not work anymore and will just stay in the house and take care of us; I was glad and thanked God for making my prayers come true.

24 I am now 15, and enrolled in Alternative Learning System.

25 I have a lot of curious questions to them but i chose to be quiet.

26 I can see that my mother was happy with Tito Fausto; I was happy for her.

27 I was also happy that I could study now; that is why i always obey my mother and we give our respect to Tito Fausto.

28 I thought that we already have a comfortable life, but I was wrong; I often saw my mother with bruises

30 I know that my mother endures pain because she does not want to go back to our previous lives, but i will do my best to protect my siblings against him.

33 He suddenly grabbed my sibling and punches him uncontrollable; I will not forgive him for hurting my youngest sibling.

35 I knew I stabbed Tito Fausto 5 times which led him to death.

36 A social worker came to me and said that he will try his best to help me.

37 Whenever I think about what happened, anger comes back.

38 I am used to live a hard life; it became easy for me to stay inside the MYRC.

39 I am always picking a fight with my co-wards just because of a little misunderstanding.

40 I am an obedient child, especially when it comes to rules and regulation of the MYRC,

41 I do not approve a bully towards weak and vulnerable children.

43 I hope the government can provide enough help to families of a CICL like me. Skills Training Programs when we got released from the MYRC, for us to have knowledge to be able to help our families.

45 I realized that anger will never be good in my life. I regret what i did and continuously pray to God that my family will still accept me.

47 My entire life is full of battle, hardship in life but I'm still standing and keep pushing to achieve my goals in life; enjoying my freedom and that is the most important.

48 I came from a broken family.

49 I am like a tree who stands all kinds of weather and keeps standings, also my mother who stands as solo parent and just like a tree who bears her fruits and taking care of it on her own.;

52 A tree is also my family who stands and stays to our mother no matter how difficult life could it who stands as solo parent and just like a tree who bears

her fruits and taking care of it on her own. be.

53 This life is challenging and full of hatred' if you choose to give up and let other people win surely you will not be successful in life.

54 I like how a tree blends and adjusts in times of challenges; I do need to do the same

Co-Researcher 5

"Innocence and Injustice Leads to Instrument of Change"

I am Jay, 15 years old. I believed in the saying, "go with the ocean wave." Sometimes, you must control your life's direction. Before my admission to MYRC, my ambition was to be a police officer. My dream/ambition as a child suddenly disappeared due to wrong justice.

I am third of four siblings. Our father was the only one to be brought us up because our mother passed away when we were small kids. When my father was getting old in age, I left him in our house with my other siblings who took care of our daily needs and the education of my siblings.

I was in third-year high school before my rehabilitation at MYRC. The school I attended had different students, which I preferred to choose for a companion. I knew they would be good to be with. However, in just a beep of a time, my life changed, which resulted from wrong decision when I chose a friend that brought me to this situation.

It started in June during the first day of class. The principal interrupted the class by introducing a new student named Ephraim, a tall guy with a thick body shape. He is a good-looking man; but my first impression of him was that of a bad boy. Ephraim came from the province. The teacher instructed to guide the new student around the school vicinity. Ephraim sat beside me. He shook hands with me and asked my name. He also asked to be friends because he has no hesitation in having a lot of friendships. I agreed because I felt he was kind, but I'm not.

The day passed by so fast. We became close friends; we shared personal matters. He mentioned that both his biological parents died already. Hence, nobody will care for him in the province. After the burial, his uncle brought him to Manila for his education. He is kind, helpful and active student. He is a fast learner; sometimes he was the one teaching difficult subjects. One time, he was absent for quite long. I became sad because Ephraim was already attached to me. After a month, he stopped his studies. I wondered why he stopped. The reason that sinks in my mind was, he went to his aunt. Suddenly someone told me he officially stopped. I really didn't know where he was staying right now. I tried to continue and not be affected by his absence. I continue to be an excellent student; I didn't want to waste the money spent on my studies. My ambition was to be a police officer. I promised to my father that someday, he will see me wearing a police uniform.

One day, while walking from school, someone called my name. He was Ephraim. I was happy to see him again. I went to him to ask how he was. He told me he stopped his studies because his aunt died. He was working, and he asked me for a little of my time. When we were in the fast-food chain, I asked him about his work, but he did not answer my question. He told me to order what I want to eat; he offered that take out some foods for my family. I was so shocked when I saw he had so much money than I expected. He also said, sometimes he will bring me to the place where he works. He brought me home and asked for my number for easy contact. When

I arrived home, he gave food to my father. My father asked me where I got the money to buy food. I told him it was Ephraim. I also told him that one day Ephraim will accompany me to his work. My father told me he already provided our needs. So, I didn't need to find a job. He warned me that the part-time job will affect my studies.

After some time, Ephraim texted me, asking how I was! We conversed through text for a long time. He convinced me to go with him to his job. I do not know about his work; but he promised to explain when I see his actual job. I asked permission from my father and my siblings because I will do a project with my classmates. On my way to the place of Ephraim, I notice how he convinced me to be with him. I told myself that this will not happen again. When I reached the place, I saw Ephraim. He had a motorcycle. I asked how far it was. He told me to get in and he will tell me when we were near our destination.

When we were approaching the place, I noticed why he was looking for someone and observing people and situation. I was shocked when he immediately snatched the cell phone off someone standing on the street. I didn't what happened next when he drives the motorcycle quick. I thought it was one time, but he did it again 3 times. We stopped at the dark and tiny street. I was so angry and walked out from Ephraim. He pulled me back and said it was only tripping. He told me to wait for a while. He went somewhere, but he left the key of the motorcycle with me and the things he snatched. I asked to be with him going to his house but he told me it can't be. While he was walking away, I was thinking about what to do. I thought Ephraim will not come back and someone will catch me. Suddenly, I saw police officers came out from the street where I was standing. They immediately arrested me for snatching-robbery. I tried to explain that I was innocent, but the officer took me to the police mobile. When I was walking with the police officers, I saw Ephraim. Suddenly, he hid in the street. I saw the two ladies whom Ephraim snatched the things. I beg to the officer and told them I was not the one who did it; it was Ephraim. I told the officer I saw Ephraim in the street, but the officer never listened to what I was saying.

When we arrived at the precinct, the two ladies provided a sworn statement to the officer. I heard the complaints of ladies. They told to the officer that they will not file a case. What was important to them was to return their belongings to them. Same thing was done by the officers. The police mentioned that holdup incidents are tolerated in Manila because there are no complainants pushing to file complaints. Hence, the complainant was forced to file a case against me. I asked for one police officer to barrow his phone just to inform my older siblings about what happened. However, after one call the police officer get his phone and mentioned that the phone is not allowed inside the cell. I didn't have any knowledge where I will be placed in prison, I cannot sleep well due to limited space.

The following day, my older sibling went to the precinct. They accompanied me to proceed to MYRC, where a Social Worker oriented me about the rules and regulation in the centre and the punishments for those who disobey the certain rules. My siblings asked the social worker how long I will stay at the MYRC. The answer was, it depends on the court proceedings. My siblings were sad and worried. What if I can't finish my studies? The Social worker mentioned that the centres have ALS or Alternative Learning Program wherein I can have a review for next year's examination. The social worker allowed me to speak with my siblings for a short time before I entered the dormitory. I was so emotional and so remorseful with what happened. But I insisted I was innocent. I was not the one who snatched the cell phone and the bag. My siblings knew I was innocent and promised to me they will do anything for my case.

It took several months before I adapted inside the centre. The dormitory is big but there were a lot of children inside. There were no comfortable beddings, it was hot and lots of mosquitos. I had always been thinking of my father and sibling's situation. Once a week they can see me here. The last time my father saw me, he was full of tears and very emotional about what happened to me. He told me to tell the truth when I was speaking with a lawyer and judge. Before they go home, I told my siblings not to bring my father again for his health.

My father and my siblings have been a significant support to me, most especially in this situation. They are my light in my dark hours which I experienced. They were my inspiration and strength as I face this problem.

My wish has been for the government to lessen the disobedient police officers. If they hear my thoughts before, maybe it was Ephraim who was here, not me. I also wish that the law will be fair to all, no matter how rich or poor.

Figure 11: Bird Symbol

I choose the Bird as a Symbol, but I can't draw it. For me, the bird has freedom and can fly where ever he wants to. Unlike me and other CICL still inside the centre, many like me are the victim of wrong system which suffers a lot. Like a bird, when in a cage, it feels pain, sadness and homesick because it cannot be with the love one and family. Like us as a social worker, we were a victim of circumstances and misleading man in position. The long stay at MYRC, I realized the relevance of following my parent' rules. If I obeyed my father's advice not to accompany Ephraim, maybe I would not have suffered this situation.

I am with my family right now and, most especially, I'm still studying. I realized it is not enough to know one person before trusting him. Because Ephraim attached to me, I trusted him very much. He convinced me easily for wrong doings.

I draw a bird. Means that freedom is all I want, not just for me but for all the victims of injustices, more so to the Children in Conflict with the Law just like me. I hate the feeling when you are deprived of your own liberty, especially when you know to yourself that you did nothing wrong. I feel those inside of MYRC who are just victims of injustices.

I like the bird because it can freely go anywhere it wants. It can fly with other birds and go to a place where nobody goes. I can compare myself to a bird which is free to go anywhere until such time he was caught and put in a cage and just like me, the same faith happens to me. I do my things and go everywhere freely and all I thought it will never end but twist of event happen and turn things into ugly phase of my life.

For me, bird not only symbolize freedom but also peace. I want to be the instrument for keeping the peace and freedom not only in my family but also in my community. I can still be a role model to other children in my own way, my style and in my will."

First Reflection: Textual Themes

1 I believed in the saying, let yourself go with the ocean wave.

2 Sometimes, you must control your life direction.

3 Before I admitted at MYRC, my ambition is to be a policeman,

4 A child with dream that suddenly disappeared due to wrong justice.

5 Our father was the only one to brought us in the future because our mother passed away when I was little.

6 my other siblings are responsible for our daily needs and for the education of my siblings

7 my life change and result to wrong decision when I failed to choose a friend that brought me to this situation.

8 He asks a request to be his friend because he has hesitation to have a lot of friendships. I agreed because I felt that he was kind but I'm not.

9 The day past so by, we became close friends and shared other personal matters.

10 He is kind, helpful and active student.

11 I became sad because Ephraim is attached to me.

12 I continue to be good student and i don't want to waste the money spent for my studies

13 My ambition is to be a police, I promise to my father that someday, he will see I am wearing police uniform.

14 I was so shack when I saw that he has so many money than I expected.

15 My father told me that he provided the needs for them that's why I don't need to find a job.

16 he convinces to accompany me to his job even though I don't have any Idea

about his work.

17 I ask permission to my father and my siblings with the reason that I will do project with my classmates.

18 I was shack when he immediately snatches the cellphone of someone standing at the street.

19 I don't what happen next when he drives to motorcycle very fast.

20 I was so angry and walk out from Ephraim, he full me back and say that was a tripping's only.

21 They immediately arrest me for the Snatching-Robbery

22 I tried to explain that I am innocent but the officer takes me to the police mobile. When I was walking with police officers,

23 But the officer never mined what I am saying.

24 My siblings felt sad and worried what if I can't finish my studies

25 I been so emotional and felt remorse for what happen. But I pin point that I was innocent and I'm not the one whom snatches the cell phone and bag.

26 My siblings knew that I am innocent and promise to me that they will do anything for my case.

27 The dormitory is big but there are a lot of Children inside the centre. There are no comfortable beddings, getting hot and lots of mosquitos.

28 my father saw me was full of tears and very emotional for what happen to me

29 I speak with my siblings not to bring my father again for his health.

30 They been a light to the darkness I experience right now and my inspiration to be strong to face the problem in life

31 government to lessen the disobedient police officers.

32 I also wish that the law will be fair for all, not matter how rich or poor.

33 the bird has freedom and can fly where ever he wants to. Unlike me and other CICL still inside the centre.

34 cause of wrong system which suffers a lot.

35 Like a bird than can be in cage, where he feels pain, sadness and homesick because he cannot be with his love one and family.

36 I realized following my parent rules is important

37 If I obey my father's advice not to accompany Ephraim, maybe I will not suffer to this situation.

38 I am with family right now and most especially I'm still studying

39 I realized that, it is not enough to know one person before to trust him.

40 that freedom is all I want not just for me but for all the victim of injustices more so, to the Children in Conflict with the Law just like me.

41 I hate the feeling when you are deprived of your own liberty especially when you know to yourself that you did nothing wrong.

42 I feel those inside of MYRC who are just victims of injustices.

43 Bird for me is not only symbolizes freedom but also peace.

44 I want to be the instrument for keeping the peace and freedom not only in my family but also to my community.

45 I can still be a role model to other children in my own way, my own style and in my own will.

Co-Researcher 6

"Facing Responsibilities through Strong Faith of Salvation and Purity"

I am Gerald, 17 years old from Tondo, Manila. I had a live-in partner before I was rehabilitated at MYRC. I am the younger of 2 siblings. My father is an employee of a private company while my mother stopped her work to take care of us. My brother is currently studying at a public school and has a scholarship while I am in grade 10 level. I was in grade 9 when Kristel became my girlfriend. She was my classmate for so long; however, my parents didn't agree with my relationship with Kristel. If they let me, it was in one condition: I will continue my studies.

Our relationship was good. After a month, they accepted Kristel as my girlfriend. If we were home early, she went to my house to do some homework. My mother saw the dedication of Kristel for study and her big dream for herself and her family. After our study together, my mother always invited Kristel for dinner before she goes home. My mother always told me not to go home late.

One day, Kristel went to school with a mark of sadness in her eyes. I asked her what her problem was. She confessed to me that her stepfather tried to abuse her sexually. I was worried. I convinced her to report the incident to the police station. She didn't want to report it to the police because she thought that her mother will never accept it. She also stated that before going to school, she tried to confess the incident to her mother that her stepfather went to her room. Her mother slapped Kristel because of the accusation against her partner. I was worried so, after school, I decided that Kristel stay at home. At our house, Kristel told my mother what happened. My parents and I brought Kristel back to her house.

We saw Kristel's mother and her stepfather in their house. Her mother was busy assisting Kristel's younger siblings. After a while, she approached to us for our concern. During the confrontation between my parents and Kristel's mother, her stepfather became angry and commanded us to get out of their house. Kristel beg to her mother to be with us and her mother allowed it.

Kristel cried until we reached home. She was so sorry for behaviour shown by her mother and stepfather. She slept with her friend but my parents made sure that she slept in our house because it was late at night. I slept on the sofa while Kristel slept in my room. The next day, Kristel wanted to get her stuff at her house, such as uniform, bag, books and some clothes. After going to her friend's house, worried about her, I accompanied her to her house. We entered her house safe, but she tried to get her needs fast because she did not want to see her stepfather again. Before bringing her to her friend's house, we ate lunch first. Kristel was so sad; she kept silence since we left their house. I kept thinking about how to convince my parents for Kristel to live in our house.

Before going to the mall, I told Kristel I needed to go to the comport room. That was the time I called my parents to allow Kristel to stay in our house. In return, we will continue our studies. My mother agreed, but we needed to talk to my father and Kristel's mother. Upon returning to where Kristel was, I told her I could convince my mother, and she agreed she stayed at home. She was shy, but she didn't have a choice because she had nowhere to go. When my father arrived from work, it did not surprise him why Kristel was still in our house. Maybe my mother told him about what happened. He told us that my mother will talk to us after dinner and it happened. My parents assured Kristel that the house was open and she was welcome. She need not pay anything. She just has to feel at home. Kristel and I promised not to break the agreement by not doing unacceptable things, for we were determined to finish our studies first.

The first one month of stay at our house has no problem. It was hard on my side because I was sleeping on the sofa since the time Kristel stayed in the house. I thought it was alright than Kristel going back to her house. We inspired each other; my parents observed and were happy that I never went out with my friends. Kristel became my inspiration and the reason I never missed school and my grades got higher.

However, as a youth, I had perspiration and pleasures. One day, we were dismissed very early because the teachers had a meeting. We went home directly. When we reached home, we opened the door softly. I thought my mother was sleeping in her room, but she was not in the house. There were no other people in our house. Because of pleasure and emotions, we engaged in sex. Afterwards, she cried. I apologized for what happened. She was scared. What if she became pregnant? I assured her she will not be pregnant. I told her to be on the sofa before mother comes back. My mother arrived shortly; she was surprised to see us home early. I told her we just arrived and the teachers have emergency meeting.

After three months, my parents noticed Kristel was getting sleepy. I told them we had loads of homework and we slept late. One day, when my mother was cooking, Kristel run to the comport room; we heard Kristel vomiting. My parents looked at me. I thought Kristel was pregnant. Afterwards, I went to buy a pregnancy test. On my way back home, I wished Kristel was not pregnant. I gave the pregnancy kit to Kristel. When she got out of the comport room, she was crying because the result was positive. My parents were so angry with us. Suddenly, they realized there was no choice but to accept the fact the Kristel is pregnant. We apologized to our parents. Kristel was so shy because my parents treated her like a daughter.

I was on one side thinking about how it happened. I can't accept at this early age that I will be a father. Even though I love Kristel, I have a lot of dreams. I truly never accept the fact that we are both minor and this is happening.

Because of the incident, Kristel had to stop going to school. She was so shy because in one month, there would be a moving-up ceremony. I tried to continue my studies, but it was really hard for me.

Sometimes, I joined a group of students who are notorious for cutting classes, trying to escape from the reality that in a month, Kristel will bear my first baby. I learned how to smoke and drink alcohol. Later on, I tried to use drugs.

Kristel and I have several fights because she knew I had been skipping classes, and I was with wrong peers. She warned me she would tell my parents had I continue doing the wrong things. Instead of saying sorry for what I did, I told her it was all because of her. I also told to her I am not ready to be a father at my young age. I added that I have so many dreams for myself and my family. I threw many words that I knew really hurt her feelings. I also told her that if my mother will know what I was doing, she will be out of my house and I will not recognize or accept the child as mine.

I was distracted when I was in class. My friends noticed I had a big problem. So, they invited me for a drink at our friend's place. During our drinking session, one of my friends brought a drug. He told me to use it just to forget my problems. In a couple of hours, the doors and windows were locked. We never knew there were police officers outside the house. When the police officers searched the house, they caught us in action using drugs. No one skipped the room because all of us were on drugs. It was my friend's grandmother who reported to the police station.

At the precinct, our parents and guardians were informed. They went to the police station. My friend's mother was crying, and the father was angry about what happened. The police officer oriented us that, as minors, we will not be put to jail; but we will be placed at the MYRC. Because I took the drug, I did not understand what was happening.

Upon arrival at MYRC, the social worker oriented us about the rules and regulations of the said centre. The Social Worker also told me I cannot see Kristel because of her condition. That was the time I realized that any time my child will be born without me seeing them. I felt sorry for what happened. I apologized to Kristel, to my parents, to my child, and also to myself.

For several days, I cried about what happened. I asked myself what happened to me and why I let this happen. I realized that whatever happens to me, I can take this and will be okay again for my parents, for Kristel, and for my child. Once a month, my parents visit me. Sometimes, Kristel is with them. They never abandoned Kristel and my child. I told Kristel, when I am discharged at MYRC, I hope she was still be at home and will accept and forgive me.

It is really hard to be CICL. There were a lot of changes in my life when I was at MYRC. I needed to be with somebody, no matter who they were. I needed to follow rules, and most especially, I needed to sacrifice because of what I did. I believe that all will be okay because my parents support me, and I am guided by our Lord, Jesus Christ. I learned the problem cannot be resolved by skipping classes or by escaping from it; but, that I should face it directly to learn and stand for who I am.

My symbol is a Rosary. I'm not a typical religious person at all, but I must admit that in my situation, with all my suffering, sacrifices, hate and bad things that I have done, I surrender everything to God. I have no one to turn to and my only hope and savior is God. I learned to submit myself to him.

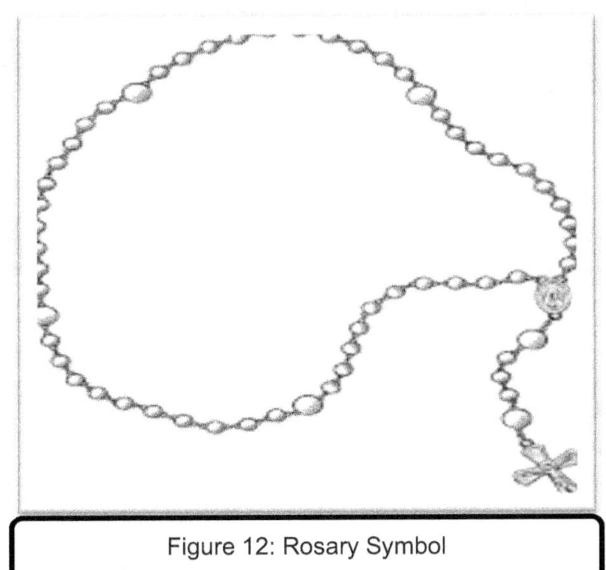

Figure 12: Rosary Symbol

Yes, life is like a Rosary, full of mystery. In each mystery, I found salvation and purity. Prior to my confinement in MYRC, I had a live-in partner who I accidentally impregnated, and later lived with me, together with my family. When this happened, I got confused and started asking myself and even God. Puzzled, I turned to friends who negatively influenced me. They were the ones who influenced me to use "Shabu" and "marijuana" to forget all my problems. The first thing that I hated was the fact that at a young age, I was going to be a father. I was afraid of the responsibility. Second, I would no longer enjoy my life because of the responsibility that goes with fatherhood at a young age. These things made me do unlawful things.

I became dependent on drugs and a prisoner until my friends and I were caught using it. In jail and in MYRC, I realized that the stupid things I did in life and I regretted it, but it was too late. This Rosary that I pray every night keeps my faith strong. I dreamt that someday I would be free, which happened. It was not too long to wait. Just like the Rosary, it moved mysteriously to get me out of the MYRC.

This life, although somehow rough and not too smooth to sail, if we have to trust the Almighty, everything will be fine. Our faith will help us understand all trials in life in mysterious ways.

First Reflection: Textual Themes

1 My father is an employee of private company while my mother decided to stop her work to take care of us.

2 my parents doesn't agree to my relationship with Kristen, they let me in one condition that I will continue my studies.

3 Our relationship became good and suddenly after a month they accepted Kristel as my girlfriend.

4 My mother always thought me not go home late.

5 she confessed to me that her stepfather tried to abuse her sexually.

6 I felt worry about what happen and I decided after school, Kristel will be at home

7 I convince my mother so that she can stay in our house.

8 We inspired each other and my parents observe and felt happy that I never go out with my friends.

9 Kristel became my inspiration and reason why I never been absent to school and my grades get higher.

10 Due to pleasures and feelings, we had been sex.

11 My mother and father were so angry to us but suddenly they don't have a choice just to accept the fact the Kristel is pregnant.

12 We apologized to our parents and Kristel was so shy because my parents treat her like a daughter.

13 I can't accept in this early age I will be a father.

14 I have a lot of dreams, I truly never accept the fact that we been both minor and this is happening.

15 I accompanied to some other group of students who was remarkable as always whom cutting the class

16 I would like to skip from the reality that a month Kristel will born my first baby.

17 I learned how to smoke and drink alcohol. Later on, I tried to used drugs.

18 Kristel and I have several fights because she knew that I been skipping class and with the wrong peers

19 I am not ready to be a father with my young age

20 I have so many dreams for myself and my family.

21 I was distracted when I go to school.

22 My friends were notice that I have a big problem

23 They caught us in action using drugs.

24 Because of drugs I intake, I really don't understand what is happening.

25 I realized that any time my child will be born that I cannot see them

26 I felt remorse for what happen, for Kristel, my parents, my child and to myself also.

27 It was several days that I am crying for what happen.

28 I realized whatever happens to me. I can do this and will be okay again for my parents

29 They never abandoned Kristel or my child

30 There are a lot of changes in my life when I was at MYRC.

31 this will be okay because my parents support me

32 the guidance of our Lord Jesus Christ

33 I learned that the problem cannot be skipping but I should face it directly for me to learned and stand for who I am.

34 All of my suffering, sacrifices, hate and my bad things that I've done I surrender it to God.

35 For no one to turn to and my only hope and savior is god I learned to submit myself to him.

36 I passed I found salvation and purity.

37 I got confused and start asking myself and even God.

38 I got puzzled and turn to my friends who negatively influenced me.

39 They are the one who makes me use "Shabu" and "marijuana" to forget all my problems.

40 I'm afraid to that responsibility at all. Second is I will not enjoying my life because of my early responsibility.

41 I become dependent to drugs and become prisoner of it until me and my friends caught using it.

42 This Rosary that I verse every night keeps my faith strong and to dream that someday I will be free which happen not too long to wait.

43 This life although somehow rough and not too smooth to sail but if we have trust to our almighty everything will be fine.

44 Our faith will help us understand all the trials in life even in mysterious way.

Researcher 7

"The Essence of Compassionate Service towards Transformation"

My experiences when handling children in conflict with the law have given me the chance to grow not only in my career as a social worker, but as an individual. I meet lots of challenges here in this institution (Manila Youth reception Center) as I handle these children. They have unique personalities, offences committed, families and behavior. All these deals with them and I have to have lots of patience and understanding towards them.

It all started when I requested my department to consider me to work an institution since I studied that time in Philippine Christian University, taking up my bachelor's degree in social work. I needed that time a night schedule to catch up with my class in the morning. So my superior decided me to transfer to the Manila Youth Reception Center.

When I started working with children in conflict with the law, it was scary, for it was new to me. At first, I didn't know how to interact with them, knowing their cases are no joke. It took me some time to understand their dynamics and behavior. My role at first in MYRC was houseparent, a surrogate parent who attends the needs of the CICL. I'm in charge of opening and closing all dorms and securing all residents.

During my first stay in MYRC, I had all the luxury of hearing all their stories; each story differs from another. All of them are victims and innocent. They were all framed by police officers, and no one believed them.

I heard one story, which I believe is familiar to me. We both became a father at an early age. The only difference is he is having a legal battle, and he is inside while I am free. Every night we talked and sometimes he cried and regrets all the wrong things he did and for not listening to his parents. Even though he is in a dilemma, I see him as a strong and brave kid. He never lost his faith in God and in his family. He even told me that his family regularly visited him, which brought him joy and hope in life to continue moving on.

The second story is that of a Muslim child who was facing a drug case which is not bailable. He admits he is guilty of the offense he committed. He did it purposely for his family; he sold drugs and became a courier for it. He had no other choice but to do it for his family to have food on the table. He said he is both a victim and a culprit. I admire him because of the way he talked; he knows everything and can handle himself properly. He leaves his faith to Allah that someday he can do better things in life when he becomes a free man.

Every night I used to listen to different stories which somehow made me the lucky person who I am. The CICLs don't want to be in their present situation. No one wants it, not even their families. But because of unfortunate circumstances that they encountered, they are in MYRC suffering.

Each individual has his/her characteristics that somehow triggered or pushed each of them to the limits, but they would not understand it. There is one instance where a newly admitted case would not want to go inside his dorm; some force and counseling were needed to get him in. There are CICLs who have a hard time adjusting inside the dorms, especially the first-time offenders and first-time to part ways from the family.

Understanding them and their legal battle in court needs a courageous social worker to help them out in this institution, I handle different cases such as heinous crime committed by CICL's for example, rape, murder and drugs which have no bail. These children have to suffer emotionally, for they are far from their respective families. As social worker, we are the only ones who they can depend on.

Handling a Child in Conflict with the Law is the most challenging work I've ever experienced in my profession as a social worker because they are difficult to handle, considering the sensitivity of their cases. Gathering information about their family background is difficult.

In interviewing, some are not cooperative and they do not provide their true identity and truthful response to questions asked of them. However, working with CICL really challenged me a lot to be a good worker because I have to be more patient, open-minded, and lenient. I have to practice being non-judgmental and accepting of all my clients.

Working with CICL also made me want to help them on their respective cases because a lot of them showed sincerity of being regretful for their offense or crime which they confessed or admitted to the private complainant and/or arresting officer/s and plead guilty to the court.

As a social worker, I monitor their behavior at the center every day. I saw changes from their admission until the day of hearing. As the time goes by and the rapport has already been built between me and my client, we can communicate regarding their case. My clients already have their trust in me, thus, each detail of the case, the true or real scenario that happened the day before the apprehension, are articulated to me. They cooperate with me regarding the data gathering for submission of the report to the court.

Each client has a background story why they did the unlawful act or the offense or the crime. According to my clients, they unwillingly do the crime due to peer pressure and poverty. They know mentally and physically the consequence of their action, but they still push through to survive from poverty and sometimes from loneliness.

Most of the cases I handled were about drugs, robbery, rape, theft, murder, attempted homicide, and gambling. It has really broadened my knowledge that, even minors can actually do a crime without hesitation. By that, I know, they need a person who they can trust and who can educate them properly so that they will not commit the same crime again. They need a person who can motivate them to change for their own benefit and for the benefit of their family, especially their parents.

In my first months as a new Social Worker, I was shocked by what I saw inside the Center. I was stunned at the thought of children from 15 to 18 years old inside the Center can do things that put them there. How did these young children get there? What are the cases they are in? I always thought about my sisters whose ages are the same as my clients. They are so young to be staying in the Center. But in my 6 months, little by little, I could understand the situation. Poverty, need for attention and love. These were the most common roots or reasons these young children ended up in the Center. Poverty is one root-cause why children do snatching in exchange of money for their family's basic needs, especially food. Need for attention and love is another reason or root case for children to spend most of their time with their peers or friends, where they receive more love and attention. Unfortunately, in most cases, they influence them to do something wrong.

Let me tell you a story about one CICL who I handled. His name is John Paul. He violated Republic Act 9165, Section 5 and 11 and no bail. He has co-accused which is his mother who is behind bars in Manila City Jail female dorm. The only means of communication between the two is through his grandfather, who visits his mother in Manila City jail and carries the letter intended for her. It happened almost 1 year ago. The minor pities himself in his situation, for he has no chance to see his mother to cry on her shoulder. His case was raffled to Regional Trial Court Branch 09, one of the family courts here in Manila, which is known for slow disposition regarding CICL cases. His grandfather seeks advice and recommendation from the Public Attorney's Office (PAO) about any legal option that they can avail for his grandson to get his liberty. Since holiday season is approaching, his public attorney advised them to move the case for temporary liberty of his grandson to be out on pass this Christmas up to New Year. He was also advised to talk to his grandson's social worker to get a recommendation for the motion to be attached as a supporting document. On my part I was hesitant to give the minor the recommendation being asked because it will be a risk on my part if John Paul will not follow all the conditions set by the Court. My license will be jeopardized if he will not return on the date that this institution set. It was the first time in MYRC that a CICL would be allowed out on pass to spend the holiday season with his family.

Being always for the best welfare and interest of the minor, I have to do my part. I recommended John Paul to spend his holiday season with his grandfather. On December 23, 2005, RTC branch 09 issued an Order of Release on Holiday season by Out on Pass CICL John Paul to his grandfather starting December 24 to January 02, 2006. I had mixed emotions about this decision. I was happy because for the first time in the history of MYRC, one CICL will spend his time with his family during the yuletide season. However, I was also afraid that John Paul will run away and will not return to this institution as agreed. As days went by, I constantly texted John Paul and his grandfather about their whereabouts and what they were doing.

John Paul maximized his very limited time to do his things with his family. He visited his mother in Manila City Jail (female dorm). His dream of being with his mother finally came true. He never missed a day visiting his mom, which made her feel that her son loved him so much. He enjoyed himself, making quality time with his siblings. Time flew so past, John Paul returned to MYRC as agreed. Upon his return, his co-residents asked him so many questions. It clearly became a motivation to all CICL that they can also be like John Paul if they will behave and if their families are very supportive of them. I made John Paul an example to all residents of

MYRC. I told everybody that even though they are in the center, there is still hope for everything. At present, John Paul is a branch manager of one producer of donut and has his own family.

I still have one more story which inspires me to work here and in dealing with CICLs. Tim is a member of LGBT community. His case was theft, and he spent 6 months here in MYRC. His mother is a teacher and came from a well-off family. He narrated he did the unlawful act purposely for his family to be aware of his behavior. His family was too busy attending to their business, and he was left alone. Being the youngest of his three siblings, he did not feel the love and affection of his family. One time, together with his friends, they took chocolate bars in '7-11' Convenient Store. He purposely did the act to be caught by the 7-11 management. He was turned over and placed here in this institution, but to his surprise, his family never visited for over a week for him. He regretted doing it and asked me to call his family to inform them they imprisoned him. I was glad his family knew his present condition, and they were preparing to visit him. Even though the

y can bail him out, his family opted that he stay and let his case be finished. His family wanted him to learn his lesson hard. Tim thought his family abandoned him and never loved him at all. His hardship inside MYRC taught him a lesson. He is thankful to his family. He considers himself still lucky compared to other CICLs. When his day of release came, his family waited for him inside the center. He hugged them and promised he will change for good. He said he clearly understood that all the things that his family was doing were all for their future. At present, Tim already graduated from the Phil. Normal University with a degree in Bachelor of Science in Education.

Not all the time, a client has a success story in MYRC. I have CICLs who are recidivist which makes me feel weak and ineffective social worker. It saddened me when one of my clients went back again to MYRC. I saw reasons the child kept coming back and kept committing unlawful acts. It was because of the poor economic condition and no family and community support from the place where he lives. These are the factors that I see why CICLs keep coming back to the center. As a social worker, I would like to say that implementing the Juvenile Justice Welfare Act, also known as Republic Act 9344, is not beneficial to our children. It has so many flaws. I will not enumerate each flaw, but all I can say is I am strongly against it.

As a Social Worker handling Children in Conflict with the Law (CICL), I need to be very understanding of the children. This is my first ever job after passing the Social Workers' Licensure Examination last 2018. I was trying to get a job in my hometown, but I was unlucky. After 6 months of waiting, I applied for a Social Worker position in the City of Manila. Luckily, I got hired. I am assigned to the Manila Youth Reception Center, a LGU-run-Institution, by the Manila Department of Social Welfare from 2019 up to present.

As a Social Worker handling Children in Conflict with the Law (CICL), I also need to have a lot of patience. As a worker who is new to the field, though I heard about South Center in my college, I was still shocked when I was in the actual situation. I had been thinking that my clients are just 3-5 years younger than I. I was not sure if they will obey me considering that they do not even obey their parents. With my first 20 clients, I just had an answer to my question.

These clients are all children. Hard-headed children are often disrespectful, but they apologize when they realize they are wrong.

As a Social Worker handling Children in Conflict with the Law (CICL), I must be tough. Social Workers like me who handle minors, we all know children are aggressive. Little things or big things, they can create trouble. There was one incident that happened inside a dorm (CICL room) where CICLs fought with each other. My co-workers and I did not know what to do except to stop them. Being outside the dorm, there was not much we could do but to scream, "tama na yan!" repeatedly. I was shocked when they stopped. So, being a social worker really needs to be tough.

As a Social Worker handling Children in Conflict with the Law (CICL), needs empathy. These children have more experience in life than I do. Some of them are no longer in school; some started working as a child in order to help the needs of the family. I cannot judge them. I did not experience what they went through. I did not stop studying. I did not work as a child. My parents have jobs to provide for our daily needs, especially education. So I don't judge them for snatching phones or for any unlawful acts they did in exchange for money to buy for the needs of their family.

As a Social Worker handling Children on Conflict with the Law (CICL), I need a lot of knowledge. In working in a case-related job, we must know how to handle not only the CICL but their cases, too. In this field, we also work with courts, Judges, lawyers. As a Social Worker-In-Charge of these clients, I submit Social Case Study Reports, behavioral reports, recommendatory reports as ordered by the Courts.

The MYRC is ageing. It was built in 1963. Its facilities are not conducive for CICLs to stay. Our total capacity is only one hundred (100), but somehow our cases here are over the total capacity. We don't have space for our recreational activity and counseling room. Our visiting place is too small to accommodate all the families who want to visit their love ones. These are the factors we clamor for. We want first to rehabilitate our institution before our CICLs. It is high time for us to improve our facility, but it's beyond our control.

I symbolize a hand as my experience working with CICL. Handling CICLs is a team approach. We have here a medical staff, house parent, psychiatrist, court social worker, and teachers from Alternative Learning System. Each one of us has a role to play. We see our residents are being taken care of and provided all the services offered by this institution.

Figure 13: Hand

First Reflection: Textual Themes

1 A chance to grow not only in my career as social worker but as an individual.

2 Deal with them and you yourself has to have lots of understanding.

3 CICL's have hard time to adjust himself inside there dorms

4 Understanding them as well their legal battle in court need a courageous social worker to help them out in this institution,

5 These children have to suffer emotionally for they are far from their respective families

6 Social worker you're the one who can defend on.

7 Minor pity himself to his situation for he has no chance to see his mother and cries to her shoulder.

8 Slow disposition of CICL's cases.

9 My license will jeopardize if he will not return on the given date this institution

10 Being always for the best welfare and interest of the minor, I have to do my part.

11 I'm happy because for the first time in MYRC history one CICL will be spending his time outside with his family this yuletide season

12 I'm afraid that John Paul will run away and will not return to this institution.

13 Even though they are here there is still hope for everything.

14 At present John Paul is a branch manager of one producer of donut and has its own family.

15 Which makes me inspire working here and dealing with CICL's.

16 There is no always success story in MYRC.

17 CICL's who are recidivist and that makes me feel weak and not effective social worker.

18 Given their economic condition and family support more so, their community

where that child lives in.

19 Implementing this law is not beneficial to our children and it has so many flaws.

20 I strongly against it.

21 Facilities are not conducive for our CICL's.

22 We don't have space for our recreational activity and counseling room.

23 These are the factors we are clamoring for us to rehabilitate first our institution before our CICL's.

24 Reform our facility but it's beyond our control.

25 Handling CICL's is team approach.

26 Each one of us has its own role to play seeing to it that our residents are being taken care and provided all the services of this institution.

My Second Reflection: Structural Themes

Structural Theme 1 – Family support: A Significant Factor of Transformation

Co-Researcher 1: "*I have responsible and hardworking parents who never neglected us and generous in complementing us for a job well done. My parents always told us to study hard because that is the only thing, they could impart to us. I adore my family because they keep me pushing to enlighten me and motivate me to continue my life without my father."*

Co-Researcher 2: *My maternal grandmother, Lola Miling, raised me all by herself. Lola Miling had to work hard for the two of us so that we will not starve. We barely had anything to eat because she was sick for several days. It was my grandmother who stood by my side and tried her best to give everything to me."*

Co-researcher 3: "I am the youngest among five children, and I am the only one studying. My parents have a stall in Divisoria where they sell fruits, vegetables, food seasoning and other items related to food. My older siblings, on the other hand, have all graduated from college and are now employed. They continued to work hard and strive each day so that they could fulfil their desire of sending me to a private university. My older siblings, however, are not so keen on the idea thus they often advise me not too drink too much. They also told me to study hard so as not to disappoint our parents. I just had to ask my older siblings and they give it to me because they are all gainfully employed and all are still single. I did not expect that they would actually buy me a brand new motorcycle. My parents have been working so hard for me, to send me to a private university and give me a weekly allowance that is more than enough. Both of my parent are hard worker who augments a living thru selling fruits and vegetables and considering that all of my siblings are working I can ask easily money for my allowances."

Co-Researcher 4: "When my father left us, my mother did everything she could to raise us. A tree is also my family who stands and stays to our mother no matter how difficult life could it be. A tree also stands as solo parent who bears her fruits and taking care of it on her own."

Co-Researcher 5: *"Our father was the only one to bring us in the future because our mother passed away when I was little. my other siblings are responsible for our daily needs and for the education of my siblings"*

Co-Researcher 6: "My father is an employee of private company while my mother decided to stop her work to take care of us. Our relationship became good and suddenly after a month they accepted Kristel as my girlfriend. My mother and father were so angry to us but suddenly they don't have a choice just to accept the fact the Kristel is pregnant. I realized whatever happens to me. I can do this and will be okay again for my parents They never abandoned Kristel or my child"

Family is where a child learns the fundamental skills of life. The family structure and family process matters. From the narratives of my co-researchers, it has been clear the outcomes for both children and adults are not equal irrespective of family background. Children who grow up in a healthy and supportive family are more likely to lead happy, healthy and successful lives than those who have not experienced the same level of family security and stability. The values, attitude, beliefs, and outlook on life of an individual are shaped by the way they are raised by the family.

Family, therefore, plays a crucial role in the growth and development of a child; the way a child behaves in and out of the family circle is an outcome of how the child is brought up. As the primary social group, the family influences the learning and socialization of a child. A child's physical, emotional, social, and intellectual development is influenced by the family since it is the first learning institution of every child. As the child develops and learns to socialize outside the family, they carry with them what they learned from the family.

In this study, what my co-researchers have become is an outcome of how the family brought them up. Indeed, family is vital to the growth of a person. It is a great support system. The family can transform a child.

Many people point out that family is the smallest group of social life. It is also the first group of people who teach a child about the crucial fundamentals of life. The family teaches norm and value of life and what is right and what is wrong. Family is an institution with the function of teaching a child from birth onwards. Also, the family instructs children and gives guidance about personal values and social behavior. Hence, family has a significant effect on family members.

Family teaches children value, attitude, belief, faith and even culture. The family could provide children a positive perspective in social life aside from providing an environment that encourages learning both at home and at school.

Family is expected to provide economic and emotional support. My co-researchers believe economic and emotional support is a function common to families. The presence of this function can lead to a child's success in any endeavor the child wants to embark on. Family is the basic foundation of society's economic institution. Economic support from parents provides children more opportunities to get better education and good social environment. Economic support is crucial to the success of a child. A family that provides for the education of children, such as school fees and material needed for learning, can expect a child to be conscientious in school and earn a degree. A family support that provides the basic needs of its members, such as food, clothing and medicine, is important. It is an essential provision for life subsistence.

The emotional support of a family is another significant factor for a child to achieve goals. Showing love and warmth to children creates happy children and family, and builds a firm foundation for joy and closeness to one another. The love of parents for children is also important because it can motivate children to become more courageous. It also inspires children to work hard and do well in the area that they want to be in the future. Thus, family support may help reduce stress and increase protection and security in a child's life.

As family is the first institution where a child learns many things about life, it is also an economic and emotional support for a child. Love, affection and inspiration from family are factors that can encourage a child to do his/her best to become successful in life. A family's support can inspire a child to aspire for success in all aspects of life, including development of positive interpersonal relationships and transformation.

Structural Theme 2 – Broken family leads to longing and loneliness

Co-Researcher 1: "Our lives changed when my father died, his death was a great loss because he was a role model to us all. We struggled when my father died and he was granted justice. I was left behind still grieving the loss of my father, and I still could not accept my father's death. I drowned myself in grief, loneliness and longing for my father. I entered the school with a heavy heart and a loneliness I could not contain. I was not interested in the succeeding classes and I just wanted to relax.

Co-Researcher 2: "I was born out of wedlock and my parents have their own families now. I never knew who my father was; he already left my mother before I was even born. I'm a product of broken family who failed to raise me properly. I was thankful to the financial help of my mother but I was longing for something more. I often asked myself if my parents ever loved me at all. I envied other children, because of the love and care they receive from their parents and other family members. Lola Miling doesn't earn much, that's why I was not able to continue my studies after I graduated from elementary"

Co-Researcher 3: "I felt bad because I did not get what I wanted this time, and I was not use to that. I know I was being irrational and selfish, but since my envy still consumed me, I did not accept any reasonable explanation or justification for not getting what I wanted."

Co-Researcher 4: I remember my parents separated when i was 7 years old. They are always fighting, to the point that my father begun to abuse my mother physically. He was an alcoholic and every time he is mad, he will hurt us and express his regret. I was also physically abused by him. I will just cry and sleeps in the arms of my mother. There are nights that i cannot stop my tears, not just because of tiredness, but also because of my mother's absence. I want mother to stop her job and just take care of us. My mother told me that she cannot support my studies anymore and to force educate myself while taking care of my younger siblings."

Co-Researcher 5: "Like a bird than can be in cage, where he feels pain, sadness and homesick because he cannot be with his love one and family

Co-Researcher 6: "It was several days that I am crying for what happen. Kristel and I have several fights because she knew that I been skipping class and with the wrong peers. I would like to skip from the reality that a month Kristel will bear my first baby.

Co-Researcher 7: "Given their economic condition and family support more so, their community where that child lives in.""

Family is the smallest, most sensitive yet important social system. Group of families comprise the larger social system. The family, being a powerful influence on the child's growth and development, and an important primary agent of socialization, could undoubtedly either enhance or hinder the academic achievement of a child depending on the social climate of the family where the child belongs.

Early childhood parental care is one of the most important factors that helps foster a child's abilities. When parents no longer love each other and decide to part ways, a child can feel as if their world crumbled. The level of anger a child feels may vary depending on the situation when the parents separated. For instance, the age of the child, how much they understand the situation and the support they get from parents, family and friends can be the determinants of the level of anger a child may feel.

Even if the parental relationship had been very tense or violent, children may still have mixed feelings about the separation. Many children hold on to a wish that their parents may get back together. Whatever has gone wrong in the relationship, both parents still have a very important part to play in their child's life.

The unfortunate reality widens the income gap in Filipino families. Educational attainment is one key area that influences family income. My co-researchers come from low-income families. They started school behind their peers, who come from more affluent families. This is shown in measures of school readiness. Incidence, depth, duration and timing of poverty have influenced their educational attainment, along with community characteristics and social networks. The limited opportunities the children have contributed to their low self-esteem and anxiety.

Loneliness is an emotionally unpleasant state that arises from a perception of a lack of desired interpersonal relationships. Adolescents are vulnerable to feeling lonely. Adolescent loneliness has been linked to the social and developmental changes taking place during this period. In particular, a growing need for autonomy and desire to establish a separate adolescent identity that stretches beyond the immediate family environment is reflected in increasing separation from parents and attempts to establish new relations with peers in the wider social world. However, disproportionate and unrealistic expectations, feelings of rejection, failure to forge social roles, as well as parental blocking of this drive for greater independence, can all result in feelings of loneliness.

Although loneliness is a universal and normative phenomenon, the experience of loneliness can take very different forms. Chronic loneliness has been linked to negative affectivity. Loneliness can be extremely painful and may cause severe anguish to a point where its consequences can even be life-threatening. Understanding which factors are associated with adolescent loneliness and how it affects well-being is essential for formulating effective interventions to deal with this phenomenon and its effects.

Emotional and behavioral problems in children are more common when their parents are fighting or separating. Children can become very insecure. Insecurity can cause children to behave like they are much younger and 'clingy.' Nightmares, worries, or disobedience can all occur. This behavior often happens before or after visits to the parent who live apart from the family. Teenagers may show their distress by misbehaving or withdrawing into themselves. They may find it difficult to concentrate at school.

Structural Theme 3 – A diversion of openness to peers to cope up in environment

Co-Researcher 1: I opted not to share my emotions to my family for fear that they may not understand me. If I hang out with a different crowd, I may be able to cope up better, the pain might easy up a bit and I may be able to get back on my feet. Hanging with the gang means escaping from reality. My friends never cared to visit me or bothered to send food or medicine when I was sick. I realized that they were with me only in times of enjoyment. I was nervous and it as not easy for me to just go inside houses and take all their stuff. I know it was wrong, I also know very well that we could go to jail if we get caught. I had no chance to run, everything happened so fast.

Co-Researcher 2: A stranger man helped me to pay our debt in the sari-sari store. I obey his order because I badly needed money. I was happy because it was my first time to see and have that much money. Though hesitant, I obeyed him because I have not saved enough money to resume my studies. I know that what I did was wrong but I promise to stop once I had enough savings to resume my studies. I was a bit worried because my grandmother might catch me if I came home too late. I felt betrayed and instantly I also felt remorseful. I did not mean to lie to my grandmother, but I am certain she will get mad and scold me if she found out the truth.

Co-researcher 3: Enrolled in a private university, I was surprised with my classmates because they are far richer than I am. Some of my classmates, those who did not talk to me before, became friendly to me all of a sudden. I might lose focus on my studies and just drive around the city or anywhere I want to go if they heeded my desire. I wanted to have lots of money like him; he is more than willing to make me his partner in selling marijuana. I did not think twice because I really wanted to buy a car someday, and not only that, I also wanted to buy more expensive stuff like clothes, gadgets and shoes that I can use in school. I could live independently, away from my controlling parents and nagging older siblings. I always thought that I might get caught on the act of actually selling marijuana by one of the roving security guards. I was hesitant the first time he invited because I did not know him that much, I felt insulted; I did not think I was too obvious, or that I was already wearing my heart on my sleeve. Things happened so quickly; the cops immediately handcuffed Rick and me I discovered that Rick is no longer a minor, and that his father is not really rich.

Co-researcher 4: I have a little knowledge of her job while talking with Aling Yolly but I'm still afraid to ask her. I have a lot of curious questions to them but i chose to be quiet. Tito Fausto answered that she will not work anymore and will just stay in the house and take care of us. I thought that we already have a comfortable life, but i was wrong. I knew there that i stabbed Tito Fausto 5 times which led him to death but i will do my best to protect my siblings against him. I am always picking a fight with my co-wards just because of a little misunderstanding. I like how a tree blends and adjust her in the times of challenges and I do need to do the same.

Co-Researcher 5: He is kind, helpful and active student. He asks a request to be his friend because he has hesitation to have a lot of friendships. I agreed because I felt that he was kind but I'm not. I became sad because Ephraim is attached to me. The day past so by, we became close friends and shared other personal matters. He convinces to accompany me to his job even though I don't have any Idea about his work. I was so angry and walk out from Ephraim, he full me back and say that was a tripping's only.

Co-researcher 6: He is kind, helpful and active student. He asks a request to be his friend because he has hesitation to have a lot of friendships. I agreed because I felt that he was kind but I'm not. I became sad because Ephraim is attached to me. The day past so by, we became close friends and shared other personal matters. He convinces to accompany me to his job even though I don't have any Idea about his work. I was so angry and walk out from Ephraim, he full me back and say that was a tripping's only.

I got puzzled and turn to my friends who negatively influenced me. I accompanied to some other group of students who was remarkable as always whom cutting the class. I learned how to smoke and drink alcohol. Later on, I tried to use drugs. They are the one who makes me use "shabu" and "marijuana" to forget all my problems.

My co-researchers are concrete thinkers. There are many gray areas on the spectrum of lying, including white-lies and lies of omission to avoid hurting someone's feelings. For those who are concrete thinkers, these nuances make it hard to learn what's okay and what's not okay for lying.

Sometimes the onset of lying is sudden and intense. It's a new thing where they were pretty truthful most of the time before and then suddenly, they lie about a lot of stuff.

Most parents think children lie to get something they want, avoid a consequence, or get out of something they don't want to do. These are common motivations, but there are also some less obvious reasons my co-researchers might not tell the truth — or at least the whole truth.

My co-researchers lack the confidence to tell grandiose lies to make themselves seem more impressive, special or talented to inflate their self-esteem and make themselves look good in the eyes of others. My co-researchers have anxiety and depression might lie about their symptoms to get the spotlight off them. They might minimize their issues because they don't want people worrying about them.

Peer pressure grows in intensity as my co-researchers move up through the grades; by the time they reach high school, fitting in has become a priority–and often a source of anxiety—too many. Since most of them are not that open to their families to discuss their problems, they are open to their peers in the school as part of coping up.

The desire to fit in and feel like being part of a group is normal, and most of them feel this way sometimes, especially in the teen and young adult years. Peer pressure, that feeling that you have to fit in, be accepted, or be respected, can be tough to deal with. It can be overt or less direct. While peer pressure can be helpful, it can also cause them to do things they may not be sure about, or even things they don't really think are right for them. Dealing with this pressure can be challenging, but it's important to reflect on their own personal values and preferences and decide based on those rather than on peer pressure.

The notion of innocence refers to children's simplicity, their lack of knowledge, and their purity not yet spoiled by mundane affairs. They were taken advantage of the surrounding people, which resulted trust issues and betrayal. They were used by the people that led them to wrongdoings. Such innocence is taken as the promise of a renewal of the world by my co-researchers. Innocence has been attributed to them and childhood by adults at all times, but content and social function of such glorifying assessments show considerable variation over time and context, and the valuation is never unanimous among contemporaries.

Managing peer pressure is usually not that difficult if people whose values, preferences, and behaviors are like them only surrounded them. However, in my co-researchers' environment, it is likely that they will meet people with a wide variety of attitudes and behaviors. It may feel easy to know where they stand and act; but at other times, they might feel confused, pressured, or tempted to act against their own judgment. Also, sometimes when they are away from home and family, they have more freedom to make their own choices. They even feel a desire to do things their family doesn't do or doesn't think are right to establish their own identity and try new things. Again, it is important to reflect on what they think is important, their values, and who they want to be.

Structural Theme 4 – Regrets and remorse an effect of wrongdoing

Co-researcher 1: *I barely passed my subjects but thankful I was not expelled because of absences and tardiness. I skipped school more than usual, because we were engrossed with selling prohibited drugs. I was tempted to give more money to my mother, to compensate for all my mistakes and offenses, a life that led me to commit offenses which I regretted later on. I was living a life which that was the exact opposite of the life I once had. I will forever remember my mother's face when she visited me inside the police station. Being a CICL was regrettable experience. I brought pain and shame to my family, most especially to my mother who has sacrificed so much.*

Co-researcher 2: I know there was nothing I can do now. I have regrets to my father and other but it doesn't make sense to keep my hated to them inside my heart. I was close to tears because I knew how much I disappointed my grandmother. I was so ashamed of what I did and I was also crying as I asked for forgiveness from my grandmother.

Co-researcher 3: The only setback was I slowly veered myself away from my family and my other classmates. I did not want to disappoint my parents and of course. I know it was a burden for my parents, physically and financially, and it was only now that I realize how much they have sacrificed for me. I was so remorseful for what I did because despite all the disappointment I gave them, they continued to support me, and they never abandoned me. I can consider it as an endless agony and pain in my life. I was ashamed because my father and my older siblings were also with her. I did not know my mother had a heart ailment, and that she almost had a heart attack when she learned of my situation.

Co-researcher 5: My life change and result to wrong decision when I failed to choose a friend that brought me to this situation. If I obey my father's advice not to accompany Ephraim, maybe I will not suffer to this situation. My siblings felt sad and worried what if I can't finish my studies. My father saw me was full of tears and very emotional for what happen to me. I speak with my siblings not to bring my father again for his health.

Co-researcher 6: I have a lot of dreams, I truly never accept the fact that we been both minor and this is happening. I can't accept in this early age I will be a father. I felt remorse for what happen, for Kristel, my parents, my child and to myself also.

Co-researcher 7: Minor pity himself to his situation for he has no chance to see his mother and cries to her shoulder

. Sometimes the choices of my co-researchers do not lead to the best likely outcome. To behave properly, they need to learn how to choose wisely. The claim that regret may play a key role in underpinning decision-making is interesting in a developmental context, because regret is considered a complex emotion that emerges relatively late in development. These considerations suggest that the emergence of regret facilitates better decision making in my co-researchers.

Regret is a negative emotion that occurs when the outcome of a decision is compared unfavorably with an alternative, counterfactual outcome that a different decision could have been made. Studies have shown that my co-researchers' regrets are averse: When making a choice, they avoid outcomes they expect they will regret. They do not describe the means by which this occurs, but they claim that the regret experienced not only helps them to remember their mistakes and missed opportunities; it also motivates them to engage in reparative action by mental undoing. It also prepares them to behave more appropriately when they are confronted with similar choices in the future.

Thus, experiencing regret leads to the evaluation and coding of a choice as a poor one and makes salient alternative courses of action. The primary means by which such emotions affect choices is by leading my co-researchers to expect negative emotions in the future and thus avoid repeating choices that would lead to such emotions.

Because regret is a counterfactual emotion that involves in comparing what is to what might have been, the ability to experience regret must develop after the ability to think counterfactually.

My co-researchers have behaviors that get them in trouble. They might tell lies or have angry outbursts, and these actions or words can sometimes be hurtful to others. When that happens, it can have lingering consequences — not just for the person who's been hurt, but also for them.

Some people may not think of children in conflict with the law as feeling remorseful for something they've said or done. But even if it doesn't seem like it, my co-researchers feel bad when they upset someone — even more so than other kids. They often have trouble managing emotions. So, feelings of remorse can be deep and have an unexpected impact on self-esteem.

Regret is when people wish they hadn't taken the action they took or said the hurtful thing they said. This is often because their action had a consequence that upsets them. While remorse is about feeling bad about having made someone else upset. It's feeling empathy for others and guilt that you've caused them pain.

My co-researchers often have difficulty with self-regulation and other executive functioning skills. They may bolt things without thinking about whether it will hurt someone's feelings. When their impulse upsets others, kids often feel bad because they didn't intend to hurt anybody.

My co-researchers have the tendency to fixate on things. Instead of apologizing outright, they may spend far too much time trying to do it just right. They might dwell on what they've done, going over and over what they could have done differently or better. Or they may lie to get out of the situation. Lying takes away the pressure of having to say sorry, which can be especially tough for kids who experience social anxiety.

All this leads my co-researchers not only to feeling remorseful but also to feeling bad about themselves. Some of my co-researchers may even feel like it's just "one more thing" about them that makes them different or not "good enough."

Shame is a complicated, intensely uncomfortable, and "sticky" emotion. It usually comes about in response to something they feel they have done wrong or reactions they have had that they feel bad about. It includes feeling exposed, unsure and sometimes humiliated and it ends up feeling like it's "who they are." In contrast to the dull ache of regret, shame has a sharp, groundbreaking that makes no distinction between reasonable and unreasonable. It makes teasing apart what they have done well, and what they might have done differently is almost impossible, as everything is thrown in the same basket and seen as bad. Their fault is unforgivable. Most parents of my co-researchers extend their heart and soul. Their actions, feelings, and experiences exposed them to feeling shame for them, about them and about themselves.

The cycle of doing "bad" things and then feeling like a "bad" person can have a negative impact on my co-researchers. It lowers their self-esteem and their motivation to keep trying. Knowing the challenges of these children allows us to help them avoid negative situations and handle feelings of remorse.

Structural Theme 5 – Supportive environment and compassionate service as part of transformational journey

Co-researcher 1: *My adviser and I had a heart to heart talk and she gives me pieces of advice. I also realized that there are people who are willing to help me. I was fortunate that my social worker is nice and he had such an impact in my life.*

Co-Researcher 2: I felt that I have more freedom to ask my social worker anything concerning my case

Co-Researcher 3: She told me, she knew how I felt, and she knew college life was hard. Instead of being envious, I should use it as an inspiration to study harder. My family still picks me up in my trying times and gives me the second chance that I don't deserved somehow. The social worker gave me the same support my parents give, and for that I am forever grateful. She also made me understand the importance of doing my best to get along with the other CICLs in the center.

Co-Researcher 4: Our neighbor, Ailing Yolly, gave some food for our dinner. A social worker came to me and said that he will try his best to help me. I thanked my social worker for always reminding me to be calm at all times to prevent a fight against other children.

Co-Researcher 6: We inspired each other and my parents observe and felt happy that I never go out with my friends. Kristel became my inspiration and reason why I never been absent to school and my grades get higher.

Co-Researcher 7: Deal with them and you yourself have lots of understanding. Understanding them as well their legal battle in court need a courageous social worker to help them out in this institution, We social workers are the one who can they defend on. Being always for the best welfare and interest of the minor, I have to do my part. Which makes me inspire working here and dealing with CICL's. Handling CICL's is team approach. Each one of us has its own role to play seeing to it that our residents are being taken care and provided all the services of this institution.

My co-researchers are less likely to develop friendships than their typically developing peers. They have difficulty with peer interactions. If they do not address these social delays and friendship skills when children are young, they are at risk of social isolation, rejection, and social-emotional delays.

My co-researchers develop social-emotional competence within the context of their relationships with their teachers, neighbor, family, and MYRC. They develop a communication style, learn socially appropriate ways of responding, and became more independent from their caregivers, families, and communities. Cultural values and priorities also drive expectations about developmental milestones. MYRC also influences parenting practices and ways of dealing with emotions, including handling stress and coping with their adversity.

The personal experiences and environmental factors that activate the physiological stress response to prolonged periods of time disrupt my co-researchers' brain circuitry and impact physiology, behavior, and health. Essentially, too many or too long stressful experiences are unpleasant for them. The statement is referring to major, lasting problems: verbal abuse in the home, a chronic lack of affection for children, physical threats to family members, and an addiction problem.

As a social worker, our role is also to model and show the values that we hold regarding relationship-based care for children and their families. Keeping the needs of the children and youth as our priority can be challenging, with so many responsibilities. Showing that the children and youth are our priority is an important way that we communicate the program's mission and value of maintaining an emotionally supportive environment. As in any family, the tone set by adults influences the growth and development of the children. As the social worker, the children, families and staff will look to us to show how to react to tough issues, decide, and interact with one another.

As the social worker, they charged us with creating and maintaining a supportive environment. Gathering feedback from staff and families about their perceptions of the program environment will be important in creating a supportive program.

Maintaining a supportive environment includes building relationships with children, staff, and families. We can do this by assisting staff in setting and meeting professional goals, welcoming and mentoring new staff members, and contributing positive comments and ideas that enhance staff members' and families' confidence and competence in their roles as caregivers and parents.

We need to set goals and develop a professional growth plan with these children to facilitate their professional development. Self-reflection is an important skill to have as a social worker. Our role is to ensure that the program is a welcoming, friendly, and emotionally responsive environment for the children, families, and staff. Our vision of a welcoming environment is clear through the care we show for the physical and emotional comfort of the children, families, and staff affects building an emotionally responsive environment that shows all are welcome in this caring community.

The first and most important strategy for preventing challenging behavior is developing positive relationships with these children.

We can encourage positive social interactions by demonstrating respect for them. This includes modeling respectful forms of communication, respecting the decisions children make, and respecting overall differences in others. We encourage these positive interactions by modeling them ourselves. Respect every staff member, including your manager, and show this respect in your words and actions.

Structural Theme 6 – Failure as an opportunity to success

Co-researcher 1: My inability to cope with the loss of my father has caused me to neglect my studies .Give us ample opportunities to prove to society that we are capable of becoming better individuals and have the ability to change for the better. CICLs and PDLs alike would be able to lead normal lives again, without being judged by other people, without being stigmatized and being treated like persons with a contagious disease. I will be successful in life.

Co-researcher 2 I was a simple boy who dreamed of becoming successful one day. I could not understand, perhaps because I only finished elementary, or because I was so confused. I firmly believe that success comes to those who work hard for it. I wanted to finish my studies and become successful someday so that I may provide grandma a comfortable life.

Co-researcher 3 I began comparing myself to my college classmates. I can't help but feel envious. I was consumed by an unbearable envy that I talked about it even as we dined that evening at home. Give importance to us CICLs that being a CICL does not define us, and that we are capable of correcting our mistakes and that we have the capacity to change for the better. Stigma end so that we can be fully rehabilitated and that we will have the opportunity to prove that we can also be productive members of the society. Up to present proving my worth to my family and keeping my right track is my priority and this circle of positive life empower me as always to strive much more harder.

Co-researcher 4 I started to read my old books while taking care of my siblings. I still want to study. I know that my mother endures pain because she does not want to go back to our previous lives, I cannot protect my mother from Tito Fausto, My entire life is full of battle, hardship in life but I'm still standing and keep pushing to achieve my goals in life. This life is challenging and full of hatred if you choose to give up and let other people win surely you will not be successful in life.

Co-researcher 5 *Before I admitted at MYRC, my ambition is to be a policeman, My ambition is to be a police, I promise to my father that someday, he will see I am wearing police uniform.*

Co-researcher 6 *I'm afraid to that responsibility at all. Second is I will not enjoying my life because of my early responsibility. I become dependent to drugs and become prisoner of it until me and my friends caught using it. I have so many dreams for myself and my family.*

Co-researcher 7 *There is no always success story in MYRC. CICL's who is recidivist and that makes me feel weak and not effective social worker. I'm happy because for the first time in MYRC history one CICL will be spending his time outside with his family this yuletide season. Even though they are here there are still hopes for everything. At present John Paul is a branch manager of one producer of donut and has its own family*

Being able to identify the silver lining in a perceived failure or missed opportunity helped my co-researchers to move on to improved things — while maintaining their self-confidence.

My co-researchers dwell on success. They are thrilled when they succeed, and they love to hear or read about stories of success or of successful people. But they realized that behind every story of success there are hundreds of failure, stories of stumbling, falling and bouncing back. Joy is only the epitome of a long process of pain, sadness, and frustration. The world runs away from our failures, but celebrates with us about our successes.

Failures and rejections often trigger painful emotional doubts about the competence and self-worth of my co-researchers. Being rejected hurts, and the physiological response it creates in their bodies and minds is akin to physical pain. When they recognize that the emotions they feel are both primal and normal, it can help them move past the ache faster.

Behind the smiling face of achievement lie stories of things broken, time lost, and wishes unachieved, and goals missed. The road to success is never adorned with beautiful flowers, soft carpets, or gorgeous sights. That is why they never tire of trying, no matter how often they fail. I always imagine success as this beautiful narrative, an epic of achievement, behind which a saga of little and big failures are hidden, told and retold, to remind us of how far you have come, what steps we have taken before we learnt how to get it, how to do it.

My co-researchers never give up- they know that pain will only abate when they reach the top of the mountain. The pain of giving up leaves more durable scars than the pain of trying again and again and again.

They build on failure, live on failure, and use failure to achieve, to succeed, and to lead. The characteristics of those-who-fail-only to-succeed are diverse. The best perspective on success is through failure. It's failure that gives us the proper perspective on success. Therefore, every failed attempt gives us a sense of what doesn't work and what should work. Failure gives us perspective. It helps us focus and home in on the right obstacles and the right solutions.

Mistakes are the imperfections that push my co-researchers to aspire to perfection. In fact, they are not mistakes. They are their life lessons about what works and what does not work. The only genuine mistake is the one from which we learn nothing.

Success is a dream. But the road to success is paved with bold moves and brave acts. We have to risk something if we want to get something. We are more vulnerable because we are exposed to danger. Yes, they are afraid; but they know that overcoming fear can only happen when they espouse it and own it; if they fall, their fear does not grow. They become bolder, braver; they are vulnerable to bigger falls but also to greater achievements. Success is a thousand failures turned into a thousand lessons that allow us to overcome fear and catch the dream as it flies by us in a dark night.

Structural Theme 7 – A program enhancement as an opportunity for transformation

Co-researcher 1: My first few weeks inside MYRC were the hardest, I had a hard time sleeping with so many teenagers inside the same small room. I became better acquainted with my new environment. Provide permanent employment to CICLs and PDL after they are leased from detention Provide technical and vocational skills for male wards to better prepare them before they are integrated to their families and communities

Co-researcher 2 Life inside MYC was not easy, I was used to an impoverished life but I found it difficult to adjust inside the center. The facilities and staff of MYRC are not enough for CICL. More institution like MYRC will be built to facilitate the increasing number of CICL

Co-researcher 3 I was not able to sleep at all during my first few nights in MYRC. I had a tough time adjusting to life inside the institution, I learned to adapt to my surroundings, to get along with all kinds of people.

Co-researcher 4 I am used to live a hard life, it became easy for me to stay inside the MYRC. Skills Training Programs when we got released from the MYRC, for us to have knowledge to be able to help our families and to provide enough help to the families of a CICL like me.

Co-researcher 5 I feel those inside of MYRC who are just victims of injustices. I been so emotional and felt remorse for what happen. But I pin point that I was innocent and I'm not the one whom snatches the cell phone and bag. I also wish that the law will be fair for all, not matter how rich or poor. that freedom is all I want not just for me but for all the victim of injustices more so, to the Children in Conflict with the Law just like me. I hate the feeling when you are deprived of your own liberty especially when you know to yourself that you did nothing wrong.

Co-researcher 7 CICL's have hard time to adjust himself inside there dorms. Facilities are not conducive for our CICL's. We don't have space for our recreational activity and counselling room. These are the factors we are clamouring for us to rehabilitate first our institution before our CICL's. Reform our facility but it's beyond our control. Slow disposition of CICL's cases. Implementing this law is not beneficial to our children and it has so many flaws.

Some recognize that children and young adults are a major human resource for development and key agents for collective social change. But it is only possible when they are involved to take part in the meaningful dialogues on issues that concern them the most. There is a need to strengthen family, school, and community–their structures and the value systems, as these provide an inclusive attitude and become role models for children. There is also a need to start collective action to address their problem and empower them, motivate them, provide them a road map for self-development so that none falls off the social security net.

Every child who comes in contact with the juvenile justice system is a child in difficult circumstances who has fallen out of the protective net at some point and has been robbed of an opportunity for a safe childhood. Children in conflict with law should be treated as children in difficult circumstances and the approach of the juvenile justice system should be aimed at addressing the vulnerabilities of children and ensuring their rehabilitation.

Comprehensive, family-centered, individually tailored rehabilitation services are critical to the children in conflict with the law in successfully achieving his or her fullest potential and transformation. The care plan must address the physical, developmental, social, psychological and educational needs of the clients and his or her family.

To provide individualized rehabilitative services for a child who is growing and changing, it not only takes a team, and it takes teams of teams. The goal of rehabilitation is to return to home but also return to school life. This not only applies to cognitive activities, but socialization, exercise, sports and family time.

Family-centered care should be the essence of the program. Clients and parents should be actively involved in decision making, daily rounds with the treatment team, and discharge planning. This approach is an essential component of the successful transition home, getting back to school and back to being with their peers, families, and friends.

The idea behind rehabilitation is that people are not born criminals; thus should be given a chance to be restored back into the society. It also prevents them from becoming recidivists. Rather than punishing them as a criminal, rehabilitation seeks, by education or therapy, to make the juvenile in conflict with law a healthy citizen of the society.

The most effective way to find constructive solutions to involvement of children in activities that violate a law is to involve children in the process of rehabilitation and not to consider them as merely 'trouble makers' or 'problem children' in need of punishment. Recognition of and respect for their rights as human being and as a child is an important first step in this direction. Thus Juvenile justice has made a departure from the criminal justice model of punishment, recognizing the negative influence of association with adult offenders and the higher possibility of reformation of children being in the growing age where their capacities are still being built and developed. Juvenile Justice adopted the path of reformation of children found to have committed an offence through various community-based reformative and rehabilitative measures and using institutionalization as a measure of last resort and for the minimum period until suitable community-based alternatives are found for them.

Structural Theme 8 – A strong faith and love to family gives hope and motivation for **transformation**

Co-researcher 1: Inside MYRC that I discovered myself. I learned that all of these have to start with me. My heart began to fill with hope, as days turned into months realizing how I miss my family so much. I learned to be friendly to the other CICLs inside the center

Co-researcher 2 I enrolled in the Alternative Learning System. I was industrious student and diligently did my homework. This experience has taught me that anything gained from any wrongdoing will not result to something good. All of my family is important to me. My family play a vital role in my life. I want to keep them, to be with them and even if we have bad memories to share with, I still want to keep them. I want to keep my family as much as I can because family is love and forever, I will be thankful to all of them

Co-researcher 3 Being a CICL has taught me that nothing good can come out from being envious. I realized, had I been content with what my parents worked so hard to give me. I also learned a very important lesson: that not everything I wanted will be handed to me on a silver platter, that I will not always be prioritized. I became appreciative of the things I have now and I am grateful for the people who continued to support me during my hardest times. Most importantly being in MYRC taught me to have stronger faith in GOD. I learned to offer everything to HIM, all my fears, doubts and small triumphs each day. I learned to pray, for forgiveness for all my sins, and to pray for salvation, not only of myself, but of my family as well. I missed my family.

Co-researcher 4 I am an obedient child, especially when it comes to rules and regulation of the MYRC, I do not approve a bully towards weak and vulnerable children. I realized that anger will never be good in my life. I know that the Lord will make my prayers and dreams come. I was glad and thanked God for making my prayers come true. I regret what i did and continuously pray to God that my family will still accept me.

Co-researcher 5 I am with my family right now and most especially I'm still studying. I realized that, it is not enough to know one person before to trust him. I want to be the instrument for keeping the peace and freedom not only in my family but also to my community. I can still be a role model to other children in my own way, my own style and in my own will.

Co-researcher 6 I learned that the problem cannot be skipping but I should face it directly for me to learned and stand for who I am. I got confused and start asking myself and even God. All of my suffering, sacrifices hate and my bad things that I've done I surrender it to God. For no one to turn to and my only hope and saviour is God I learned to submit myself to him. I passed I found salvation and purity. This Rosary that I verse every night keeps my faith strong and to dream that someday I will be free which happen not too long to wait. This life although somehow rough and not too smooth to sail but if we have trust to our almighty everything will be fine. Our faith will help us understand all the trials in life even in mysterious way

Co-researcher 7 A chance to grow not only in my career as social worker but as an individual. These children have to suffer emotionally for they are far from their respective families

My co-researchers resist change unless there's a force or motivation that pushes them to do something different. Change often comes with the risk of failure or harm. The greatest changes require the greatest risks. Therefore, they also demand the most courage and motivation.

Sometimes obstacles to change build up, even if just in their minds, to where they really can't take the first step toward change on their own.

My co-researchers have people in their lives whose love will give them the courage and motivation they need to take steps toward change — people who love them as they are, but who also want to see them make the changes necessary to live up to their full potential.

Family motivation to change can best be understood as the combined forces operating within a family guiding it towards maintaining survival in the face of serious threat, and towards healing when a threat is removed. My co-researchers discovered that the force driving a family towards health is the same force that drove them to the initial adaptive behavior where a family member becomes addicted to keep the family close, preventing them from feeling the pain of intense loss and sorrow.

My co-researchers realized that their family motivation enhances their change and transformation in part by providing energy, but not by reducing stress. Their supporting family provides a powerful source of motivation that can boost their performance in the agency, offering meaningful implications for research on motivation and the dynamics of work and family engagement.

Love is one of the most powerful motivators for change. True love can give them the courage to take the risks they need to change. True love refuses to give up, even in the face of failure or hardship. It loves. This type of love from another person is one of the most powerful forces in the world, but I think there is one force that is even more powerful: the love of God. My co-researchers strongly believe there is a God, and the most powerful being in the universe loves them. Religious belief is one of the most important and belief systems a person may be motivated to adopt and maintain.

My Third Reflection: Essential Insights/Postulates: Elements of the Eidetic Insight

Brokenness Leads to Grief and Longing for Openness

Grief is a natural response to loss. It's the emotional suffering we feel when something or someone we love is taken away. Often, the pain of loss can feel overwhelming. My co-researchers experienced all kinds of difficult and unexpected emotions, from shock or anger to disbelief, guilt, and profound sadness. The pain of grief also disrupts their physical health, making it difficult to sleep, eat, or even think straight. These are normal reactions to loss—and the more significant the loss, the more intense their grief will be.

My co-researchers' condition are caught up in rumination about the circumstances of death, worry about its consequences, and excessive avoidance of reminders of the loss. Unable to comprehend the finality and consequences of the loss, they resort to excessive avoidance of reminders of the loss as they are tossed helplessly in waves of intense emotion.

Bereavement is one of life's most tough challenges, yet most people weather its storms, comforted and supported by close companions. My co-researchers find themselves stalled in acute grief that seems to persist without respite, lasting years, or even decades after a tough loss. There is a pressing need for health and mental health professionals to learn to recognize and treat people with this condition.

Grieving is a highly individual experience; there's no right or wrong way to grieve. How we grieve depends on many factors, including our personality and coping style, our life experience, our faith, and how significant the loss was to us.

Inevitably, the grieving process takes time. Healing happens gradually, it can't be forced or hurried and there is no normal timetable for grieving. It's important to be patient with ourselves and allow the process to unfold naturally.

But grief isn't some evil force that's only there to cause pain. Grief is escorting up an even deeper feeling - a truth about our life, what we value and what we need. Perhaps how much we wanted something, how deeply we care about someone, how far we've come from where we were.

Not that their grief and their faith should be separate. What is important to remember is that the depth of their grief does not imply a loss of faith. Experiencing grief does not show a loss of faith.

It is important to remember that grief is about their own experience of loss; it is not a pain or sympathy for where their loved one is. It is perfectly reasonable that one believes their loved one is in a better place, and still to feel overwhelmed with the pain of being separated from them. Further, one can believe in a greater plan while still experiencing the pain of their absence. It is not selfish to grieve; it is not a loss of faith. It is a normal reaction to a devastating situation that can co-exist with the comfort of one's faith and spirituality.

My co-researchers realized a great lesson to be learned from this longing in the way they think they should feel. That lesson is a lesson of accepting the way they feel, however that way is. When they accept the way they feel, they open up the possibility of feeling happy with it and also they give opportunity to feeling something different. If they have a predetermined longing to feel a certain way, then they close their mind to the endless possibilities that are out there. When they truly accept the way they feel and are happy with that, then I think they are making progress towards their transformational journey.

Supportive and Compassionate Service towards Transformation

A variety of influences that can have both positive and negative effects complicates the experience of my co-researchers. It has shown that economic hardship is associated with dysfunctional families and with a range of difficulties for my co-researchers, including risk-taking. This sort of stress is likely to have a negative effect on parenting, yet positive parenting can also profoundly affect outcomes for my co-researchers. They also tend to seek peers like themselves and to become more like the peers with whom they associate. The net effect may be positive or negative.

Similarly, strong bonds with teachers and peers at school can be a positive influence, but many characteristics of my co-researchers are not conducive to the development of such bonds. Communities also may have structural characteristics that are supportive of positive adolescent development—such as social networks and resources for them. Finally, the rapidly expanding universe of media devices and venues have a profound influence on the experience of my co-researchers, with effects that include developing norms for many behaviors at the same time the media provide a potentially powerful tool for influencing them in a positive direction.

Compassionate care delivery enhances my co-researchers' satisfaction and quality of life and reduces their anxieties. Based on my co-researchers, because of the compassionate service of social workers, it increases their motivation to change. Various strategies are needed to improve compassionate care service.

Human behavior is complex and that in order to increase the understanding of how we can promote behavior changes, considerable efforts are still needed. There are several adjustments to be made to improve on the identified methodological weaknesses as well as developing the design of the actual interventions. Guiding children's behavior is an important aspect of educating and caring for children. Positive strategies need to be developed to assist them in learning ways of behaving.

Social workers guide their behavior through their interactions and communication at all times. The service's approach to behavior guidance in daily practice affects the learning outcomes of my co-researchers. From their experience, it shows that quality learning environments and sensitive, nurturing adults are essential for achieving positive learning outcomes for them.

When a social worker adopts a positive and active approach to behavior guidance, they reduce challenging behaviors and encourage them to achieve success, develop positive self-esteem and increase competence.

A positive, inclusive, and active approach includes considering the reasons for their challenging behavior, not just dealing with the behavior itself. Supportive learning environments need to be vibrant and flexible spaces that respond to the interests and abilities of each child. They cater to different learning capacities and learning styles and invite children and families to contribute ideas, interests, and questions.

The absence of a warm and trusting relationship with an adult often results to a child resisting direction from that adult. Both the behavior guidance practices and the educational program need to meet the developmental and individual needs of each child.

Regrets and Remorse a Motivation to Change towards Success

There are many types of regret. It can include loss, anger, shame, past relationships, or sadness. Rethinking and regretting can cause anxiety. By causing this anxiety, it leads my co-researchers to make even worse decisions that they regret. By examining themselves and seeing what they feel, they will better control these emotions and put them behind them. The past is the past and evidently cannot be changed.

One of the most important senses my co-researchers possessed is pain. Pain allows them to learn quickly from their mistakes. Without the pain, they would not learn through their failures. Without this failure, they would not learn how to succeed.

The goal created by my co-researchers is just as important as the plan to reach it because it sets the tone for their mindset. It is counterproductive; they framed it to their success if the goal is set with negativity.

If their motivation is fueled with self-loathing, then every minute spent towards their resolution reinforces this negative perspective. Failing to meet the goals they've set for themselves can act as reinforcement to their feelings of inadequacy, pushing them further into a self-destructive mindset.

The agony of regret is pointless if they cannot take from it a positive lesson that enables them to transform their life in some meaningful way. Mistakes are the greatest teachers they ever receive in life; but seeing their lessons can be hard beneath the deep layers of hurt their regrets and disappointments inflict.

My co-researchers experience regret and it can be a very important lesson and tool for their future. The important thing to take away from their mistake is how they can move past it. They use their knowledge to hustle their way to the top. They strive to succeed, no matter how much the world fights back.

Self-blame and their inability to shake off regret can affect their well-being, more than they can imagine. Instead of spending their time brooding on past decisions, regret can be an optimistic force in my co-researchers' life. It helps them to understand experiences and avoid future mistakes. They acknowledge the thing they wish they've done differently, without fixating on it, and use it as a motivator to make changes.

My co-researchers could identify and address their weaknesses. They acknowledge their weakness and use their mistakes as a teaching tool. They forgive themselves and bounce right back. Rather than letting their regrets hound their ambitions, they transform them into motivators by accepting them and moving on with a few simple tactics.

In a world with so many varying opinions, values, beliefs, and lifestyles, many of us are quick to judge the actions of others. But before we can do that, we need to be able to properly judge ourselves. We have to take the time to listen to our inner dialogue and understand where it's coming from. Our brains are wired to avoid things that cause us pain. We instinctively want to protect ourselves. We should do a better job of helping this voice be heard regularly.

Regret is one of the most miserable feelings known to man, but it's also one of the most powerful weapons in our arsenal. When we learn how to face our regret openly and honestly and accept our mistakes for what they are, we can turn our regret into inspiration.

Transformation with Faith, Hope and Love

Faith, hope, and love are the three core realities of existence. Reflecting on the meaning these realities have for us today, my co-researchers gain a deeper understanding of them as they consider them in their interrelation, rather than separately.

In real life, every time my co-researchers face unfortunate events such as setbacks and illnesses, they think God has forsaken them and no longer protect them. They can sink into negativity and lose their faith in God. Yet, as long as they pray to God in these situations and understand His will, their mistaken viewpoint is turned around.

Therefore, at all times, setbacks and trials are what they need in their spiritual life. These are God's greatest love and salvation for them. These experiences can make realize their impurities in their belief in God, and understand that these unfortunate events befalling them do not mean that God has abandoned them; instead, they should consider it God way of purifying and perfecting them.

Fragmentation, crisis of identity and meaning, touch the lives of my co-researchers. Yet the potential for growth and transformation inherent in life's struggles and breakdowns evades most of them. They realize dark times condition them and invite them to a transformed identity through deeper faith, hope, and love. Fragmentation is the underside of solidarity-communion with one another and also with our planet earth. In fact, nature is a paradigm of the process of inner transformation which brings them to the more of themselves.

My co-researchers allow themselves to imagine they deeply believe within them that there is a power that can heal and inspire them to create their desired future. If they lack faith, they will need encouragement and belief from others to hold them up and to help them take the next step, or believe them when they are in doubt.

Faith is more communal than they might think. Therefore, faith isn't just an individual act, it is communal. It is in this community that they find the strength to keep believing and to keep walking by faith. The gift of faith is that which allows one to walk boldly for God. It might be coupled with the gift of healing, or the gift of speaking or interpreting tongues. It is knowledge of knowing beyond any doubt that even the smallest amount of faith can move mountains.

So living a new life means that they strive to be renewed in the way they think and act. It means seeking the grace of the Holy Spirit to help them make these changes. Deep inside, they were all searching for meaning. When they try to fill this void with futile goals and hope, they let them down. If they remain bound in the limitations of their own thinking, they will eventually come up short and be left feeling anxious and discouraged.

Nothing lasts. Everything fades away because everything is temporary. Things change and move. All fade, but these three things remain: Faith, Hope, and Love, because they are the three components of transformation. In a world where everything fades away, transformation is everything.

Eidetic Insight

Figure 14: My Eidetic

***"Love is the foundation and purpose;
Faith is the route of attainment, and
Hope is the mindfulness to move forward
without resolution towards a
second chance for transformation"***

Expounding on my Eidetic Insight:

For treasures and blessings that this life offers, love is the greatest of them all. We live to love more than we love to live. Therefore, it is critical for us to master this beautiful and sweet art of love. If we don't, we can't be truly happy and fulfilled.

When we understand the enormity of what this means, our entire life changes because we are now in the flow of what soul is and what soul does and the entire point of our being. Our purpose is love. Our purpose is to love. Our purpose is to be loved. This means we can no longer go around spewing hate toward ourselves, towards others, towards the earth, towards God.

It means that we cannot go on hating what we do; we cannot go on doing our daily activities or doing things that do not foster love, that do not bring about love for ourselves, for others, for our planet and for our Creative Source.

Our purpose is love. Because of this, we are unlimited in ways we express it. We can express it through any endeavor we seek to do. Love causes no harm, does not set conditions, does not deprive and punish. It teaches hard lessons; it excludes the needs of other living things. All we have to do is love our actions, thoughts and words. Our words, thoughts and actions must not cause harm to anything that exists. When we step into an understanding that our purpose is love, we step into the truth of our limitlessness.

When we think of goal setting facts, we think of systematic approaches to planning. Accepted goal setting techniques may include the need to analyze, choose, justify, implement, monitor, and refine. However, important as these are, we should never overlook the importance of faith. Not blind faith, but that which inspires commitment and enthusiasm.

When problems come into our life, faith responds by defending us, and that's a good thing. We need this kind of faith, but goal setting is the opposite, and also needed, type of faith challenge. Goal setting works in the offensive and seeks to move our life forward.

Faith is complete trust or confidence in someone or something. It is a state of mind which can lead to belief in a thing. Faith alone, however, must be built through a course of action. Repetition of affirmation of orders to your subconscious mind is the only known method of voluntary development of the emotion of faith.

A mind dominated by positive emotions becomes a favorable abode for the state of mind known as faith. When dominated so intensely, it may, at will, give the subconscious mind instructions, which it will accept and act upon immediately. Faith is the only agency through which the cosmic force of infinite intelligence can be harnessed and used. Faith can help us make it through the difficulties as a work in accomplishing our goals.

Everyone thinks of hope in a positive light, something that nurtures and cultivates, but the shadow side of this positive state of being has helped my co-researchers persevere through difficult times. We're pulled out of the present moment; instead we focus on their attention, their thoughts and feelings, on some set of variables that have not yet come to pass and maybe never will.

The remedy, therefore, from the existential mindfulness perspective, is not to eradicate hope since it obviously has a lot of desirable properties and can be the impetus for productive growth oriented behavior as we construct the futures we want for ourselves. The remedy is to make sure we consciously ground ourselves in the present as we look forward to the future with hope. We don't let ourselves get lost in the fantasy; we don't let ourselves downplay what's going on around us, but commit ourselves to the cultivation of gratitude and mindfulness in daily life so that we can experience life fully instead of placing it on the back burner. When we put gratitude and mindfulness front and center, we become truly happy right now, which is really what's at the bottom of all hope. Hope is the desire to be happy. With the application of mindfulness, happiness is available right now, which makes hope secondary rather than primary, an important consideration but not the central sustaining force of life.

At the core of human experience is the ongoing work of life – the search for meaning, purpose, and belonging. The only enduring answers to the eternal quest are faith, hope, and love. In this study, I discover how the faithful are finding their way. If God is love, the key to better understanding God is to better understand what love is. The concept of love, is very much like the concept of the divine, and the enigmatic physical phenomenon of gravity, are virtually impossible to define. Yet, my co-researchers' experiences are related to the concrete and physical that help me better understand the abstract and spiritual.

Essential Implications to the Social Work Profession

The social work profession is committed to the values of human dignity, personal autonomy, self-realization, and self- determination. These are the very areas that are severely damaged in the life of my co-researchers in this study.

In the social work profession, it is imperative that the following core values are integrated to provide effective and holistic approaches to helping children in conflict with the law.

Respect for Dignity: "We must respect the inherent dignity, worth, beauty and creativity of each child."

Respect is important in social work. Respect should not be confused with obedience or tolerance, but efforts should be placed on learning to understand the child to create a respectful, professional relationship.

Many children in conflict with the law who we work with receive very little respect in their social encounters because of the sin they committed, clothes they wear, the way they talk, or their inability to read and write. I am a witness to the way they are treated, discriminated against and belittled daily by shop assistants, bank clerks and other professionals who should know better. Respectful behavior cannot come easily to people who are almost never shown it themselves.

Establishing a respectful relationship with a child in conflict with the law is therefore imperative not only to increase their self-worth but to encourage them to engage in societal services. It is the starting point for social inclusion. Using discretion and theory and communicating with that individual enables to find out mutually respectful boundaries.

Through practice and observation of those who I respect, there are some basics to establish a respectful relationship. Listening to the child is very important. In doing so, one must be honest and open so they know what actions are taken and why. Acknowledge the power difference between you and be clear from the start of what your role is and what your role is not.

Gaining respect should remain a fresh challenge for every new child we meet, which must begin with us, as social workers, being respectful to them.

Nurturing Relationship: "We believe that meaningful and nurturing relationships facilitate transformation and personal growth of a child."

A child's experience of being nurtured develops a bond with a caring social worker. This nurturance affects all aspects of behavior and development. If the social worker and the child have strong, warm feelings for one another, the child will develop trust towards their social workers who provide what they need to thrive, including love, acceptance, positive guidance, and protection.

Building a nurturing, close relationship involves a lot of tender, loving care. The basics include being loving and affectionate with the child, understanding and responding to their needs, doing things together, talking, being involved in their activities, and being aware of their friendships and interests.

We should also have programs and initiatives that support parents as they work to develop close, nurturing relationships with their children.

Most important, recognize that opportunities to connect with a child are ever present. Sometimes a sports outdoor activity, summer camps, outings, or a mountain climbing can spark conversations that help social worker and the child stay in tune with each other.

Improving clients' relationships with social worker has important, positive and long-lasting implications for both client and social development. Solely improving clients' relationships with their social workers will not produce gains in achievement. However, these children who have close, positive and supportive relationships with their social workers will attain higher levels of transformation than those children with more conflict in their relationships.

Chapter V

CREATIVE SYNTHESIS, IMPLICATIONS AND POSSIBILITIES

This chapter presents the creative synthesis and possibilities of my study. The creative synthesis is the integration of the lived-experiences of former children in conflict with the law. I based the possibilities on the analysis and reflections of the lived-experiences and insights of my co-researchers' experiences.

Creative Synthesis

Figure 15: Creative Synthesis Symbol

The creative synthesis of my study is described and demonstrated by the image below. I expound below the meaning of each aspect in my creative synthesis:

Figure 16: The blackbird

The bird symbolizes the children in conflict with the law, who seek freedom and a brighter future. Their ability to soar high into the sky is taken to be anything from signs of freedom to transition towards transformation. Many stories and folklore suggest that birds were taken as signs of renewed life, like the experiences of my co-researcher having a second chance. Seeing a blackbird for most is a sign of a good omen. Apart from being a good omen, it could also refer to a heightened awareness either spiritually or in our personal life, just like what happened to my co-researchers journey. It could also imply shyness and insecurity, which directly implies lack of self-confidence that signs of weaknesses of these children because of the limited opportunity for growth.

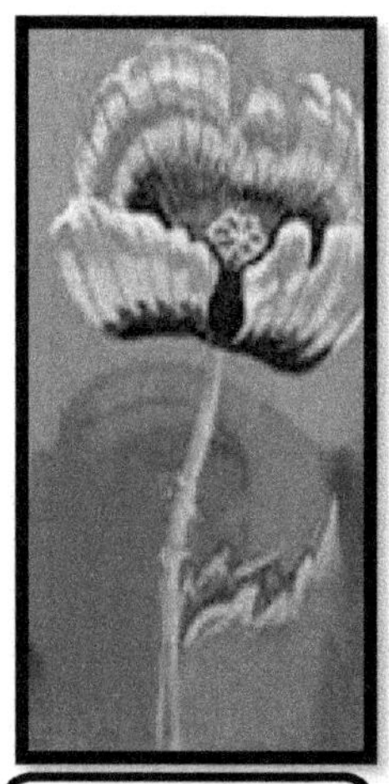

Figure 17: The flower

The meaning of flowers is an extensive process of symbolism. No one flower means family, nor does any flower have just one definition. Rather, they are a collection of thoughts, ideas and symbols for things that remind you of a family such as love, community, home and life. Therefore, in this creative synthesis, the flower symbolizes the love and support from the child's environment, including its family and community.

Providing a supportive environment is a prerequisite for fostering sustainable and well-rounded child development at an early age. To fulfill children's unlimited learning potential, they need places where they feel relaxed, respected, and encouraged to develop and gain new skills. This is a primary aspect at home, in a preschool and a community. It is especially vital to ensure children's needs in the childcare context are consistent with the care kids are provided at home, so that they feel no conflict in nurturing.

Despite of experiencing broken family relationship, my co-researchers could grasp and value the existence of supporting environment they had. They used these factors as part of their motivation to change and reach their dreams towards a successful future.

The serpent is one of the oldest and most widespread mythological symbols. They are associated with treachery because of the way they hunt their prey and their evolutionary relationship to us. In my creative synthesis, I used the serpent as the symbol of the people who took advantage of the vulnerability and innocence of my co-researchers. There were people who led and influenced them to commit a crime against the law. Many serpents are ambush-predators, which mean they use the lack of awareness of their prey to their advantage like a traitor who appears to be losing to a particular side. My co-researchers feel anger and betrayal from these people and developed mistrust to others.

A serpent uses venom to help kill their prey, rather than overwhelming it with pure force. Just like from my co-researchers experiences, they were groomed in the ways of easy money and established good relationship before they were led to commit a crime such as selling drugs and robbery

Figure 18: The Serpent

Figure 19: A Hand with Sun Symbol

The symbolism of the hand is rich and varied. In my creative synthesis, it symbolizes the social worker who provides intervention and services to the children in conflict with the law. Social service interventions comprise casework and therapeutic services design to provide child and family counseling and family support.

The hand with a symbol of the sun signifies the symbol of wisdom and enlightenment provided by the social worker during the intervention phase of the helping process to the children in conflict with the law. This wisdom gives the children a barometer on how to make good choices based on truth and not just on fleeting emotion towards transformation.

With the palm upward it represents unlimited giving, which means the social worker do everything to the best interest of the child and willing to sacrifice themselves just to provide social justice and restoration of their worth and dignity.

Figure 20: The Apple

The apple has a complex symbol, with a variety of meaning and incorporated in a variety of context. It symbolizes love, knowledge, wisdom, and compassion. In my creative synthesis, since the social worker is holding the apple and feeding it to the bird who is the children in conflict with the law, it signifies the provision of love and knowledge with compassion. It's not enough for the social worker to provide just an intervention and services to these children, but it also needs a fruit of compassion in the delivery of intervention.

Figure 21: The Growing Plant

This plant symbolizes growth and development, just like the opportunity given to children in conflict with the law. It is an opportunity to continue to bloom and grow as an individual with worth and dignity. It is important to give them the possibility to learn and see good models of life, trusting them and loving them for what they are and what they are capable of made it possible for them to change their lives and to prove that children like them deserve another chance.

Second chance is though one of those things that are easier said than done. It takes incredible patience, like the patience needed to see a growing plant. It takes some serious willpower to not get flustered. We need to find their inner strength so that we'll forever be in awe.

Theoretical Implications

In his *psychosocial stages, Erik Erikson* said people progress through a series of stages as they grow and change throughout life. During each stage, people face a developmental conflict that must be resolved to develop the primary virtue of that stage successfully. He was interested in how social interaction and relationships affect development and growth.

Most of my co-researchers are in the developmental stage. It is the stage where they experience confusion in their identity. This is the fifth stage of the ego, according to psychologist Erik Erikson's theory of psychosocial development. This stage occurs during adolescence, between the ages of approximately 12 and 18. At this stage, my co-researchers tried to explore their independence and develop a sense of self.

Maturing slowly, my co-researchers have limited opportunity of receiving guidance from their family because of the broken relationship of their parents. Their financial and emotional support from their families is very limited, which could be a factor that hindered their development at this stage.

Now, my co-researchers continue to grow physically, cognitively, and emotionally; they slowly change from being a child into an adult. Developing more advanced patterns of reasoning and a stronger sense of self; they seek to forge their own identities, develop important attachments with people other than their parents. This period can be stressful for my co-researchers, as it involves new emotions. There is a need to develop new social relationships, and an increasing sense of responsibility and independence. Trying to be independent but lacking guidance and support from parents made them vulnerable to the influence of other people who took advantage of their vulnerability and innocence.

The Pavlovian theory called *Classical Conditioning*, is a learning procedure that involves pairing a stimulus with a conditioned response. In the famous experiments that Ivan Pavlov conducted with his dogs, he found out that objects or events could trigger a conditioned response. The experiments began with Pavlov showing how the presence of a bowl of dog food (stimulus) would trigger an unconditioned response (salivation). But Pavlov noticed the dogs associated his lab assistant with food, thus creating a learned and conditioned response. This was an important scientific discovery.

There are three stages of classical conditioning; and at each stage, stimuli and responses are given special scientific terms. Before conditioning, the unconditioned stimulus (UCS) produces an unconditioned response (UCR) in an organism. In basic terms, this means that some people in the environment, like their peers and strangers, have produced an unlearned behaviour/response, such as robbery and selling drugs. Therefore, it becomes a natural response which has not been taught. In this respect, my co-researchers have not learned new behaviour yet, but they were introduced to such.

During the conditioning stage, a stimulus which does not produce a response is associated with the unconditioned stimulus at which point it now becomes known as the conditioned stimulus (CS). For classical conditioning to be effective, the conditioned stimulus should occur before the unconditioned stimulus, rather than after it, or. Thus, the conditioned stimulus acts as a type of signal or cue for the unconditioned stimulus.

During this stage, my co-researchers' behavior is associated with criminal offenses such as robbery and selling drugs frequently, or on trials, for learning to take place. However, one trial learning can happen on certain occasions when it is unnecessary for an association to be strengthened. After the conditioning, the conditioned stimulus (CS) has been associated with the unconditioned stimulus (UCS) to create a new conditioned response (CR).

The implication of classical conditioning in the social work profession is the need for service providers to make sure that children associate positive emotional experiences with learning. If the children associate negative emotional experiences with the agency, then this can obviously have poor results, such as creating a phobia.

Operant Conditioning by B.F. Skinner is a *classical conditioning* that can only be used to re-train reflex behaviours and lead the individual to produce them in response to a new environmental stimulus. However, what if a behaviourist needed a child to produce a response that was not a part of his or her repertoire of reflex behaviours? Operant conditioning would be used.

B.F. Skinner developed the theory of operant conditioning — the idea that behavior is determined by its consequences, be they reinforcements or punishments, which makes it more or less likely that the behavior will occur again. Skinner believed that the only scientific approach to psychology was one that studied behaviors, not internal (subjective) mental processes.

His idea of the behavior modification technique was to put the subject on a program with steps. The steps would be (1) to set goals that would help determine how the subject could change by following the steps. Next, would be (2) to design a program that could help the subject reach the desired state. This reflects the behaviourist viewpoint that not only can behaviour be explained by examining the environment, but that by changing the environment; the person's behaviour can be altered.

In behavioral psychology, reinforcement is a method of increasing the likelihood of a behavior. Positive reinforcement is an additional stimulus that encourages certain behavior. This is a type of operant conditioning.

Negative reinforcement is sometimes misunderstood as punishment. However, in this case, the word "negative" is not referring to something bad; rather, to the removal of a stimulus. With negative reinforcement, the stimulus is unpleasant, encouraging the behavior by its absence.

If something is being added because of a behavior, then it is an example of punishment. If something is being removed in order to avoid or relieve an unwanted outcome, then it is an example of negative reinforcement in action.

The implication of this theory is how to facilitate behavior modification to children in conflict with the law in the agency. When introducing a new positive behavior, it could be best to start off with a continuous schedule, the gradually over time shifting into one of the partial reinforcement schedules. The advantage of partial schedules of reinforcement is that they can prevent the reward from losing value too quickly. When the reinforcer is presented too often and too easily, it may lose its reinforcing power. It is a good idea to gradually wean off the reinforcer until, ideally, the desired behavior is performed without it.

According to the *Social Learning Theory*, the proponent, Albert Bandura, posits juveniles learn to engage in crime in the same way they learn to engage in conforming behavior through association with or exposure to others. In fact, association with delinquent friends is the best predictor of delinquency other than prior delinquency. The *Modeling Process* developed by Bandura helps us understand that not all observed behaviors could be learned effectively, nor learning can cause behavioral changes.

In this study, I found out that social interactions and individualism are the factors behind the juvenile delinquency. Usually, society does not exist as an island, but a unique person interacts; this ensures that the society continues to exist. The social interaction theory and juvenile delinquency have been written extensively over the years and the studies have proved logically consistent and also useful in providing the empirical support.

Thus, studies in this regard, play an important role in explaining all social behaviors without which it is impossible to explain the causes of juvenile delinquency. The primary aim of social learning theory is to explain how such social influences as religion, family and politics shape my co-researchers. This theory assumes that interplay exists between an individual, the environment, and delinquent acts.

In his *Family Systems* Theory, Murray Bowen said, even when people feel they are disconnected from members of their family, the family still has a profound impact on their emotions and actions- whether positive or negative. A change in one person can spark a change in how other members of the family unit act and feel. Though interdependence can vary between different families, all families have some level of it among the members.

Dr. Bowen believes perhaps humans evolved to be interdependent on family members to promote cooperation among families that are necessary for things like shelter and protection. But, in stressful situations, the anxiety that one person feels can spread among family members and the interdependence becomes emotionally taxing rather than comforting.

Parenting and family influences developed into a key piece of the impact family systems have on the emergent of my co-researchers. Parents play a key role in raising a healthy child by providing love, safety, and security. My co-researchers encounter experiences of parenting stress at various levels while fulfilling parenting duties in their daily routines. Parenting stresses can have factors relating to the temperament of a child, such as child behavior problems and low levels of social support. The concept of stress having a negative influence on parenting strategies supports the impact of parenting stress on the young child's development, which can have a potentially unfavorable outcome on children's behaviors and actions.

Parenting behaviors and parenting styles serve as predicates of stress on the family system. The importance of social communication provided by parents was interconnected optimistically to the potentially important information about the communicative functions of verbal communication and problem-solving strategies of their children.

The family system theory associates parenting and marriage within the structure of families in a hierarchical group with parent-child and sibling dealings. A cultural practice in family unit conversations that included spoken disagreement involving parents and an adolescent may also be considered. The study showed that clashing opinions, conflict, and concern are emergent in social phenomena and that family rules and accepted practices based on belief systems are learned through a socio-enlightening position and outlook.

According to the *Moral Development Theory* of Lawrence Kohlberg, children with conduct disorder represent most children in conflict with the law. The poor moral competence mediates the association between conduct disorder and antisocial behavior. Kohlberg's theory proposes three levels of moral development, with each level split into two stages. Kohlberg suggested people move through these stages in a fixed order, and that moral understanding is linked to cognitive development. The three levels of moral reasoning include pre-conventional, conventional, and post-conventional.

The concepts of 'liability age' and 'capacity responsibility' have been widely dissected by researchers in various fields. However, their application to both criminal and distort liability of children remains inconsistent. Rarely has an interdisciplinary approach adequately dealt with these concepts and their impact on legal norms. This endeavour to improve the applicable legal norms is supported by an analysis of the pertinent findings in psychology, particularly regarding the moral development of children. This theory serves to assess the impact of concepts of moral responsibility and maturity, in relation to the development of the legal norms, which determine the age of liability of children.

Although moral development of children has long been ascribed predominantly as an effect of parenting, there has been little systematic examination of the specific nature of this relation. I consider the implications of my analysis for teaching parents to influence positively their children's moral development. Throughout human history, communities have been concerned with the type of person who children have become. The role of adults in children's moral development, especially parents, has been a central focus.

Training programs for parents are important to include in the treatment of non-compliance, aggression and other externalizing problems in children. These behaviorally based psycho-educational programs must be designed to teach parents principles of effective behavior management, including, but not limited to, the proper use of reinforcement and punishment and guidelines for clear communication. This model could also work well in teaching parents how to foster moral and pro-social behavior in their children.

In the theory of strengths-based approaches for working with individuals, I believed that social work and human service professionals can see great outcomes when they work with the inherent strengths of individuals, family groups, and organizations. Whenever we, social workers, assist people in their recovery and their empowerment, our commitment to build on these inherent strengths goes a long way. As a social worker, I often wonder why clients seem to blossom with every change. My co-researchers pick up their bits and pieces and reconstructed hope for the future.

Strengths-based practice is a collaborative process between the person supported by services and those supporting them, allowing them to work together to determine an outcome that draws on the person's strengths and assets. It concerns itself principally with the quality of the relationship that develops between those providing and being supported, as well as the elements that the person seeking support brings to the process. Working collaboratively promotes the opportunity for individuals to be co-producers of services and support rather than solely consumers of those services.

I think the advantage of the strength-based approach is that it enables social worker to build a caring relationship with clients. It encourages social workers to convey a message of being there for a person with unconditional trust, love, and a sense of compassion. A social worker who looks beneath a person's negative behavior and sees the pain and suffering does not take the person's behavior personally. They actively listen to and get to know the talents of people and convey the message that they matter.

The strengths-based approach focuses on setting up relationships based on mutuality, affirmation of human dignity. It recognizes the power inequality between client and social worker and holds that social workers must change the way they think about clients. The strengths-based perspective favors an inductive approach, whereby insights emerge through the relationship with the clients and the stories they tell.

The basis of the strengths-based perspective is grounded in human beings' natural potential to grow and heal, on their capacity to identify wants; on the strengths of the person and environment. The theory views the person as rational and self-determining, and able to make his or her own choices and decisions. Also, it holds each person responsible for his or her own behavior and recovery. It also shows the client can only do this with the intervention of the strengths-based social worker. The social worker trusts the client, explores and discovers what the client wants, uses the client's own words, makes an assessment and reaches mutual agreement.

Possibilities

Based on the findings, reflection, and insights, the following possibilities are given for:

Schools to recognize the underlying need for belongingness as a profound force in life for children in conflict with the law, schools may more intelligently respond. School curricula could keep children grounded in a positive social network. It's not enough to support self-esteem that feeds significantly on their overall morale. If there's too much competitiveness, even winners may end up feeling left out even as they get that brief flash of achievement. Remember the need for balance. There must be more social experiences, clubs, and after-school activities to provide a child with more opportunities to feel their belongingness. There has been an insane over-valuing of individual academic achievement. While I don't discount academics, they just don't take root in the mind and soul of a child who is in a marginal or gross deficit of strokes. Children with good grades are getting depressed and we need a better way to diagnose what this is about.

Teachers need to be smarter and more sensitive to the needs and situation of their students. They must learn how to de-stress their students, handle their trauma or refer them to professional who can help them.

The theme, "*the world needs you,*" must be emphasized as a general motto, especially to children; but, all ages need to hear it. We need to elaborate and develop this theme. It focuses on the ways anybody can find a niche. We need to give more priority not just vocational guidance, but also 'avocational' guidance. I envision several classes a year, probably the middle part of the year, being devoted to identifying special areas of talents and interests of young children. Most people don't appreciate what children are good at, and what they do naturally well. A corollary, of course, is that folks enjoy doing what they do most easily.

Differences, weirdness, and oddness appear as if most people are odd in certain ways. Teachers need to celebrate this by re-framing it as a virtue, as part of individuality, as a channel for one's special function in the world. This also fits with an interesting paradox: People feel more belongingness when they can feel that their differences are enjoyed or at least tolerated. This reflects another need to discover and follow individual differences, even in the face of their having little to do with the benefit of the family or group. Attention needs to be given to reinforce children when they give themselves. There needs to be that inter-personal reward, not so much an approval that says, "*That's good*!" for it can mislead; but it could be more of a thoughtful expression of how useful, helpful, and effective it was.

Encouragement is an art, a skill. Great hosts and hostesses, like teachers, know this intuitively. It's more than mere flattery; it is a capacity to identify some positive behavior and draw it forward. Encouraging the child is a profound principle, a skill of nurturing of the active aspect of belongingness.

Government: Law enforcement mus try to ensure 'children in conflict with the law' are protected, and they receive services either through specialized shelters and other social services or through child protective services. A better approach to addressing children's need for services would be to continue developing specialized shelters equipped to handle their needs. The child must have access to a full range of counseling and treatment options, including 24-hour supervision and one-on-one monitoring. But the services are offered within a purely rehabilitative setting, and without the permanent stigma associated with being adjudged as an offender.

Federal law and international protocols have treated children in conflict with the law as victims across the board. However, not all these states have enacted immunity provisions that prevent these minors from being prosecuted for criminal offenses, while they are considered victims. The Philippine Government has also failed to enact protective response laws that provide a child protective response, rather than a juvenile justice or criminal response, for these young offenders. To ensure that these children receive services and support that reflect their status as crime victims, the Philippine Government should also enact safe harbor laws that direct these children into a child protective services framework. If the government is serious about protecting these children in conflict with the law and prosecuting those who exploit them, then enacting an immunity provision is a step in the right direction.

Church: The religious community plays a vital role in shedding light on the phenomena of children in conflict with the law. Maybe a young runaway goes to someone in the church. Maybe someone in a church has been educated and they then get in contact with authorities on this issue.

Therefore, Methodists, Baptists, Anglicans, Catholics, or anyone professing to follow Christ must continue to speak publically and intelligently against children in conflict with the law and promote health and safety measures that do not further endanger children's lives. But again, to do this, Christians need to leave their ideological and political agendas at the door and examine the depths of what Scripture, medical science, and social science must say about child offenders.

Churches may provide basic personal items and toiletries for vulnerable children and offer volunteer medical and health personnel from the church to a clinic serving children in depressed communities. They could also report signs of exploitation of minors to authorities and bring awareness of the children in conflict with the law issue in public schools to aid in prevention.

A meeting of community church leaders and interested people of faith could be started. The meeting could aim to consider how to collaborate for awareness, prevention, and intervention in their community. They can also possibly begin an outreach program in their depressed community areas, build relationships and establish presence of God in the place.

The church is most effective in doing things that bring hope and healing through God and life-changing ministry to victims.

Knowledge about children in conflict with the law framed in compassionate concern for children within our churches and communities can open doors for dialogue with vulnerable children and teens, thus making potential victims less at-risk for future offenses. A healthy identity in God and an understanding of one's value as a child of God could create good purposes for the greatest deterrents to exploitation.

The church could provide this healing journey with the patient and people of faith who believe in God's work for the life of children in conflict with the law. People believe in miracles and know that God does not anyone to perish without Him. Sadly, what society offers in terms of victim services often takes weeks. Who better to walk with child offenders than the community of faith who prays, trusts, and loves healing journey? When social services stop, who will be there for them?

Helping children in conflict with the law requires an engagement of the whole gospel. Sometimes we view ministry to those children strictly as compassion ministry or a humanitarian endeavour of the church. Helping CICLs find new life requires the whole ministry to which God has called the church a transparent presentation of Jesus as Savior, Lord, and Healer integrated with Christ's compassion expressed in practical ways to children in conflict with the law.

The spirit-empowered church is uniquely equipped to facilitate healing for children in conflict with the law. Thus, it is the work of the Holy Spirit through His people in discernment, wisdom, healing, faith, and deliverance that is critically needed to help these children to find deliverance and freedom. May God give His church wisdom and courage to engage in this battle for freedom.

Family is one of the most important sectors that can protect children. Hence, a family could create an environment where the child feels comfortable talking with them. Open communication is key. Parents should share the dangers of peer influence on their children and encourage them to alert their parents when they feel uncomfortable in any situation. Parents should trust people with whom their child interacts with, which is crucial in protecting their safety.

Parents should take time to monitor what their children do on the Internet. It is an important step in keeping their child safe. If something does not seem right, parents should ask question to their children. Parents need to establish an on-going dialogue with their child; it is critical in protecting them.

Community and its members have a part to play in properly identifying and responding to children in conflict with the law. A terminology that accurately depicts these children as victims will lead to their identification by first responders as victims of exploitation. In this sense, they could readily disclose information about their exploitation when they are addressed as survivors. Putting a single label on the crime allows multiple agencies, communities, and regions to track effectively, conduct research, and intervene in a single coordinated effort.

A **child** deserves freedom from exploitation. A first step that can be taken as a member of the community is to move this liberation forward to change the perception. Through careful use of label that we apply to children, stigma and judgments are avoided.

Police: The police department has undergone a significant shift in its philosophy of policing related to children in conflict with the law. The police should view children who are exploited as victims, not criminals. Rather than arresting them, they should provide such kids with the needed extensive services. Our police must focus on adults and predators who use these children in the most heinous ways for financial gain.

Health Professionals could collaborate with individuals and organizations that provide direct services to children in conflict with the law. They could provide efforts to prevent children in conflict with the law by identifying contributing factors, recording magnitude and health effects of the problem, and assisting children who are from depressed communities. They can also help governments, UN agencies, and non-governmental organizations (NGOs) to implement policies, laws, and programs to prevent children in conflict with the law and mitigate its effects on children's health.

Children have the right to be protected from exploitation. If they committed an offense, they still have the right to receive necessary health services. These rights will never be fully realized until there is the political will to enforce laws and fund services. Health professionals have critical roles in developing this political will.

I propose that health professionals collaborate with NGOs, governments, and UN agencies to establish an International Campaign to Prevent Child Prostitution. For this campaign to be successful, it will require global coordination, implementation at national, regional, and community levels, and the leadership of many health professionals.

Non-Government Organizations (NGOs): There are limited non-government agencies that integrate rescue operations to their programs and services. If only there are many NGOs that provide rescue operations to the children in conflict with the law, it could lessen and save many innocent children at risk. Local, national, and international strategies should be developed and implemented to rescue these vulnerable children. Once these children are rescued, they need sustainable medical and psychological support and opportunities for schooling or vocational training. Programs to rescue children and provide them with sustainable services should be assessed and details of successful programs should be shared.

Social Workers need to be knowledgeable about the characteristics, after-effects, and treatment strategies relevant to this issue, if they want to be effective in identifying and helping children in conflict with the law. Intervention activities should ideally include the child, the "silent partner," and the perpetrator. Intervention activities may also include referral to appropriate individual and/or family counseling services; securing emergency shelter, if necessary; referral to medical and legal services; and advocacy for clients. Because it is a very complex issue, the social worker needs to coordinate with an array of community services.

Social Workers could incorporate individual therapy of children for their empowerment, affirmation, and unconditional acceptance. In addition, social workers could make children know they are not to blame and allow them to learn about healthy boundaries with others. The sooner a child receives therapy, the better. This could also help them cope with the realities. A self-help and support group may be formed and used as part of group work interventions.

Asian Social Institute to continue promoting its vision, mission and goals of total human development for it opens a door for growth and self-transformation amid adversity.

Future Studies: I would propose the following studies: (1) *Peers Exploiting Friends to Engage in Criminal Offense.* This is a study that could help us better understand the different factors and perspectives that influence them to commit offenses; (2) *Adults Who Exploit Young Children to do Criminal Offense for Money and Gifts*. This future study could make us understand the phenomenon deeper and identify their inner desires that could eliminate this kind of exploitation.

The future studies cited above are significant and may use a multidisciplinary approach. It is with fervent hope that actors in the juvenile justice system could coordinate, collaborate and cooperate to work together to implement measures and uphold the principle of restorative justice for the children in conflict with the law.

EPILOGUE

Phenomenology is a complex social and philosophical theory that has direct application to a broad range of social science research topics. It requires curiosity, passion and commitment to undertake such research; the rewards are bountiful, both personally and academically. Just like my co-researchers, I have also experienced their transformational nature. By sharing my own lived experiences in undertaking a phenomenological research, I intended to encourage other students to consider the possibilities of phenomenology as a method.

In researching this topic, I found a gap in the social work literature about children in conflict with the law experiences but this knowledge gap has strengthened my commitment to the topic, and my chosen method, to use children in conflict with the law lived experiences and stories to represent their experience of their journey of transformation.

Storytelling, as a research method, facilitated the experience of sharing stories of these children. As a qualified social worker and a neophyte researcher, I had previously observed, facilitated and taken part in individuals and groups where these children had shared their stories using creative writing and art symbolism. It has provided me an opportunity to explore lived experience, and bring closer the broader context of the social world.

In developing the framework and guide questions for the research, I widely searched and read to collect detailed information and knowledge on phenomenology. There is much to read about phenomenology, particularly in the early days of trying to grapple with key concepts and their translation into research design. There are distinct schools of phenomenological thought; I was continually questioning myself, seeking understanding and clarification of whether I preferred the traditions, views and methods of Husserl or Heidegger, or descriptive or interpretive phenomenology, in the development of my research. In the end, I chose phenomenology as a method in the research as it allowed inclusion and acknowledgement of children in conflict with the law lived experience, meaning-making and knowledge constructions, as well as a representation of these within the research process.

Phenomenology embraces the value of researching children's individual experience, personal knowledge, and the representation of meaning in data analysis and transcription. By undertaking the research, my understanding and interpretation became more tangible. Sharkey

(2001) describes this process of development from a conceptual and philosophical précis of phenomenology to a stage of engaged research, as part of the individual journey of developing and designing the look, shape and feel of one's research.

There were two significant underlying reasons for me to undertake this study. First, it is my primary motivation to conduct this study to show my passion and dedication to provide high quality and effective interventions to people who are in need by inspiring and helping other professionals to be more conscious about the phenomenon of children in conflict with the law.

Second, the number of children-in-conflict with the law, either in institutions or those undergoing diversion/intervention programs in the community, has become increasingly alarming over the years. This motivated me to make this study. Since I have become part of the agent of change in helping these children, I observed that the number of CICLs have continuously risen, and more minors were admitted to the center. Some of them, after being released from the center, either on bail or through diversion, have committed the same offense after barely a month. This made me realize that there are programs and services lacking that need to be delivered for holistic transformational change of the children.

I believe it is not just my expansive reading about phenomenology, but also my personal experience with the topic that has influenced my understanding of many aspects of my research. Within the 'Heideggerian' thought, I presume that reducing our understanding to an aim opinion, bracketing out all prior experiences and emotions, we ultimately bracket out the meaningfulness of the experience we are trying to explore; we de-experience our experiences and de-world the world we encounter (Safranski,1998: 146). Heidegger's perspective was that there is no pure, external vantage point from which to get a presupposition less, disinterested angle on things (Guignon, 1999: 5–6).

Reflecting on my research, and making the choice to use phenomenology, I can see that my personal experience has played a beneficial role. It has assisted not only my understanding but also the development of my information collection tools through the provision of insight into appropriate and effective questions; interaction with my co-researchers, as they appreciated talking to someone who 'understood' as well as an increased awareness of the significance of these children's experiences, and my increasing self-awareness. This was prevalent in many interviews where a comment resonated with mine; but was especially prevalent when interviewing a child with a very similar background to my own. Our shared feelings opened my eyes and inspired me to look at further sampling and gathering information in a different light.

My experience allowed me to empathize deeply with the stories of my participants. Although some participants had similar experiences just like mine, I also found it very interesting to talk to the children who had a unique experience. This further developed my understanding of the phenomenon, as it was made more apparent to me that not only were there positive and negative experiences but also nuanced degrees of peers and community that influenced their levels of participation and understanding.

Because of my social facts, I realized there were a variety of ways that these children experienced within to engage in criminal offenses, as well as within my role as a researcher. My research journey, upon reflection, was not just one where I was encountering my participants' lived experiences, but was also one that encompassed my own experiences.

It has been of significant benefit for me to form a relationship with a more established and experienced researcher in phenomenology. It is this presence of colleagues that are interested in phenomenology that makes a phenomenological study possible; not only through academic and professional guidance, but also through personal support.

BIBLIOGRAPHY

BOOKS

Adams, Kate, Brendan H. and Richard W (2008). *The spiritual dimension of childhood.*

Anthony M. (2007). *Perspectives on children's spiritual formation: four views*. B&H Publishing.

Arksey, H. (1996). *Collecting Data through Joint Interviews. Social Research Update*, Issue 15 Winter. Guildford: University of Surrey.

Bain, K. (2009). *Parental Responsibility. Social Work and Society.*

Bala, N. (2002). Juvenile justice systems: *An international comparison of problems and solutions.*

Batson, C. & Ventis, W. (1982). The religious experience: *A social psychological perspective*. New York: Oxford University Press.

Benson, P., Roehlkepartain P. and Hong, K., (2008). *New Directions for Youth Development: Spiritual Development*. San Francisco, CA: Jossey-Bass.

Best, R. (2000). *Education for Spiritual, Moral, Social and Cultural Development*. London: Continuum.

Best, S. (2002). The community of intimacy: *The spiritual beliefs and religious.*

Bosacki, S. (2001). "Theory of mind" or "theory of the soul?" *the role of spirituality in children's understanding of Minds and Emotions*, Spiritual Education.Brighton: Sussex Academic Press, 156 –169

Bradford, J. (1995). *Caring For The Whole Child: A Holistic Approach To Spirituality*. London: The Children's Society.

Brett, R. (2002). *Juvenile Justice, Counter-Terrorism And Children in Disarmament Forum.*:29-36

Chell, E. (1985). *Participation and Organization: A Social Psychological Approach.* London: MacMillan.

Coles, R. (1990). *The Spiritual Life of Children*. Boston, MA: Houghton Mifflin.

Costache, M.P., Coman, V.L., and Matei, D. (2010). *The Liability Limits for the Minors' Acts and for Persons with Particular Legal Situation. Aspects of Comparative Law.* EIRP Proceedings.:128-132

Cullen, S. (2006). *Passion and Power.* Turin: Killynon House

Cullen, S. (2005). Kids behind bars why we must act: *A Global Report into Children in Prison.* Guildford: Jubilee Action.

Dinkler, M. (2011). *Telling Transformation: How We Redeem Narratives and Narratives Redeem Us.* Word & World31, no. 3, 2011:287-296

Flores, M.L. (2010). *Movements in the Construction of the Right to Early Childhood Education: Historical And Current.*

Healey, R. and Hinson S. (2017). *The Four Faces of Power.* Berkeley, CA: Grassroots Policy Project

Hinson S. (2016). *Worldview and the Contest of Ideas.* Berkeley, CA: Grassroots Policy Project

Hopkins, P. and Bell, N. (2008). *Interdisciplinary Perspectives: Ethical Issues and Child Research.* Children's Geographies, 6, no.1

Jensen, E. and Jepsen, J. (2006) *Juvenile Law Violators, Human Rights and the Development of New Juvenile Justice Systems*

Morris, A and Maxwell, G. (2003). *Restorative Justice in New Zealand, Restorative Justice and Criminal Justice*, Hart Publishing, Oxford, pp. 257-271

Muncie, J and Goldson, B. (2006) Comparative Youth Justice SAGE publications

Roberts, A. R. (2005). *Juvenile Justice Sourcebook*: *Past, Present and Future.* Oxford University Press. New York.

Savage S. (2006) *Making Sense of Generation Y: The World View of 15 to 25 Year-Olds.* 1st edn. London: Church House Publishing.

Sivakumar, S. (2003), *Access to Justice: Some Innovative Experiments in India.* Windsor Yearbook of Access to Justice. 239-25

Tonry, M. and Doob, A. (2004). Y*outh Crime and Youth Justice: Comparative and Cross National Perspectives in Crime and Justice*

Wahhab, M. A. (2009). *Theory and Practice, Strengthening Governance through Access to Justice.* PHI Learning Pvt Ltd, New Delhi, pp. 17-26

Wahhab, M.A., (2014). *Legal Issues in Implementing the Community Service Orders for Child Offenders in Malaysia*. Asian Social Science. 10(4):93

Yusof, W.B. and Rahim A.A. (2014). *The Age of Criminal Responsibility from the Perspective of Malaysian Shariah Law. Asian Social Science.*

PROGRAM AND RESEARCH REPORTS

Abitria R.A. (2011). *Child Protection in the Philippines: A Situational Analysis, Save the Children, the Priorities of a Youth Justice System: A Critique of the Philippine Juvenile Justice and Welfare System.*

McGill University Faculty of Law (2012). *The Unfinished Philippines Juvenile Justice Puzzle: The Missing Normative Piece to Restorative Youth Justice Legislation.*

Philippine National Report (2005). *Follow-Up to the World Summit for Children Committee on the Rights of the Child Session Consideration of Reports Submitted by States Parties Article 44 of the Convention Concluding Observations.*

Philippines Donor Report (2009). *The Italian Government: Construction Of Facilities for Children in Conflict with the Law Final Report.*

Save the Children (2004). *Guidelines for a Community-Based Diversion and Prevention Programme for Children in Conflict with the Law*

Save the Children (2009). *Research on the Situation of Children in Conflict with the Law in Selected Metro Manila Cities, Save the Children, 2004 Seed Of Hope: Learning From Programs for CICL of Partner Organizations.*

The Office of the United Nations High Commissioner for Human Rights (2016). *Children Deprived of Liberty.*

UNICEF (2005). *Justice for Children: Detention as a Last Resort. Innovative Initiatives in the East Asia and Pacific Region.*

UNICEF (2006). *United Nations Children's Fund, Juvenile Justice in South Asia: Improving Protection for Children in Conflict with the Law.*

UNICEF (2008). *United Nations Children's Fund, Justice for Children in Afghanistan Series, Social Investigation Report: Understanding Children's Circumstances*

UNICEF (2009). *United Nations Children's Fund And The United Nations Office on Drugs and Crime, Justice in Matters Involving Child Victims and Witnesses of Crime*

UNICEF (2009). *A Protective Environment to Prevent and Respond to Abuse Exploitation and Violence against Children in the Philippines, Donor Report for the UK National Committee*

UNICEF (2009). *The Philippines: Continuing Child Detention with Adults in Police Lockups, Arbitrary Detention of "Rescued" Street Children and Extrajudicial Execution of Children Accused of Violating the Law, United Nations Committee On The Rights of the Child Sessions, Briefing Paper, By Coalition To Stop Child Detention through Restorative Justice.*

UNICEF (2011). *United Nations Children's Fund, Child Protection Section, Administrative Detention of Children: A Global Report.*

UNICEF (2015). *Philippines: Evaluation of the Intervention and Rehabilitation Program in Residential Facilities and Diversion Programs for Children In Conflict with the Law.*

United Nations Children's Fund (2010). T*oolkit on Diversion and Alternatives to Detentio*n,

JOURNAL

Aala K.D. (2013). *Intervention Programs on Juvenile Delinquency Asian Academic Research* Journal of Social Sciences & Humanities, Volumes 1 issue 15

Clinton, J. (2008). Resilience and recovery. international journal of children's spirituality, 13, no. 3, 2008:213-222

Fisher, John W. (2000). *Being Human, Becoming Whole: Understanding Spiritual Health and Well-Being.* Journal of Christian Education 43, 2000: 37-42

Kerley, K. R. (2005). *Religiosity, Religious Participation, and Negative Prison Behaviors*. Journal for the Scientific Study of Religion44, no. 4, 2005: 443-457

Khan, B.U. and Rahman, M.M. (2009). *Local Government Level Restorative Adjudication: An Alternative Model of Justice for Children in Bangladesh*. commonwealth journal of local governance.:26-45.

Konar, D. (2005). *Juvenile Justice as a Part of Child and Adolescent Care*. Journal of Indian Association for Child and Adolescent Mental Health.:1

Watson, J. (2006). *Every Child Matters and Children's Spiritual Rights: Does the New Holistic Approach to Children's Care Address Children's Spiritual Well-Being*? International Journal of Children's Spirituality 11, no. 2. xv., 2006: 251-263.

INTERNET SOURCES

Ahon sa Kalye Ministries (2015). http://www.ahon-sa-kalye.4t.com/catalog.html, http://www.geocities.com/ahon_sa_kalye/org.

Cabildo, J. (2016). *Alternative Learning Gives Children in Conflict with the Law: A Second Chance* https://verafiles.org/articles/alternative-learning-gives-children-conflict-law-second-chan

Cullen. S. (2008). Criminal justice and immigration act. *Ending the culture of violence.* http://www.preda.org/main/archives/2010/r10082501

Defence for Children International (2015). http://defenceforchildren.org/files/Kids Behind-Bars.pdf

Hicap, J. (2018). M. *Govt's Cradle for Child Offenders*. http://www.manilatimes.net/

PREDA (2016). *People's Recovery Empowerment and Development Assistance* http://www.preda.org

Sunstar (2015). *Lawmaker Admits Ph Has No Facilities for Child Offender* https://www.sunstar.com.ph/article/1784081

UNCRC (2017). *The Convention for the Rights of the Child* article 27 http://www.crin.org/docs/resources/treaties/uncrc.asp#Twenty_seven

UNDP (2011). United Nations Development Programme. http://hdr.undp.org/en/media/HDR_2011_EN_Tables.pdf

UNICEF (1998). Innocenti Digest, Juvenile Justice http://www.unicef-irc.org/publications/pdf/digest3e.pdf

UNICEF (2015). United Nations Children's Fund. http://www.unicef.org/infobycountry/philippines_30525.html

UNODC (2012). United Nations Office on Drugs and Crime. http://www.unodc.org/documents/justice-and-prison reform/UNODC_Prison_reform_concept_note.pdf

UNODC (2014). *Protecting Vulnerable Children in Criminal Justice Systems in East Asia and the Pacific* https://www.unodc.org/southeastasiaandpacific/en/2014/11/violence-against-children/story.html

White, S (2001) *Handbook of Youth and Justice. The Mental Health Implications of Imprisonment for Public Protection* http://www.scmh.org.uk/pdfs/In_the_dark.pdf

LAWS, REGULATIONS AND ADMINISTRATIVE ORDERS

1989 *United Nations Convention on the Rights of the Child.* U.N. General Assembly. Document A/RES/44/25.

2006 Republic Act 9344 or the "*Juvenile Justice and Welfare Act of 2006*".

2006 *Implementing Rules and Regulations of* RA 9344 issued by the Juvenile Justice and Welfare Council (JJWC)

2006 *Manual for Measurement of Juvenile Justice Indicators*, United Nations Office on Drugs and Crime,

2006A.M. No. 02-1-18-SC entitled "*Rule on Juveniles in Conflict with the Law*" issued by the Supreme Court

2006 *Juvenile Justice and Welfare Act* (RA 9344),

2007 *Guidelines for Social Workers in the Handling and Treatment of Children in Conflict with the Law, Department of Social Welfare and Development*,

2007 *Guidelines in the Commitment, Detention and Release of Children in Conflict with the Law*

2008 *Prosecutors' Manual on Handling Child Related Cases Entitled Revised Standards on Residential Care Service* (Supplemental Guidelines on Administrative Order No. 11 Series of 2007) Amended Standards for Community-based Services (Administrative Order No. 1 Series of 2010) *Bahay Pag-Asa: Transition and Rehabilitation Home For Disadvantage Children*

2008 *Guidelines for Media Practitioners on the Reporting and Coverage of Cases Involving Children Revised*

2009 *Police Manual on the Management of Cases of Children in Conflict with the Law*

2009 PNP *Simplified Rules in the Apprehension and Investigation of Children in Conflict with the Law Guidelines in the Conduct of Diversion for Children in Conflict with the Law, Department of Social Welfare and Development*

2010 UNCEF Regional Office for CEE/CIS Criteria for the Design and Evaluation of Juvenile Justice Reform Programs, UNODC

2010 UNICEF Guidance Note for CEE/CIS on *Consulting with Children in Juvenile Justice Programming*

2011 *Standard Office Procedures in Extending Legal Assistance to the Children in Conflict with the Law* (CICL) under Republic Act No. 9344 and Other Related Laws, Public Attorney's Office,

2012 RA 10630, Amendment to RA 9344, 2012 *Revised Rules and Regulations Implementing Republic Act No. 9344 as Amended by RA 10630 A Comprehensive National Juvenile Intervention Program Framework, Juvenile Justice Welfare Council*

2014 *Revised Rules and Regulations Implementing Republic Act* No.9344, as amended by R.A. 10630 issued by the JJWC Republic Act 10630 or "*An Act Establishing a Comprehensive Juvenile Justice and Welfare System, Creating the Juvenile Justice and Welfare Council Under the Department of Social Welfare and Development, Appropriating Funds Therefor, and for Other Purposes*."

Appendix A:

ACTIVITY – SELF-NARRATIVE REPORT/ART SYMBOLISM (ENGLISH INSTRUMENT)

Objectives:

To express their own perspectives and identity

To share their stories without any judgments

To provide information that can be used to understand the purpose of existence.

To understand the lived experiences of children in conflict with the law

Instructions:

Make sure that your materials are complete such as pen, paper and art materials before you proceed in the activity.

You may start by introducing yourself (Anonymous) or can begin with your perspectives in life. In your paper, you may write your experiences as a CICL.

You may write your stories and experiences during your life as a CICL. This may include the changes/adjustments of your life after MYRC.

You may write the stories about the things that gives you motivation and inspirations in life.

You may also express your recommendations to the government and other agencies that may contribute enhancement of programs and services towards transformation.

At the last paragraph of your narratives, you may express your reflections about your experiences.

You may draw in a paper about a symbol of your experiences as a CICL. Please explain to the social worker/facilitator about your symbol interpretation.

1. After you write and draw your lived experiences, you may submit it to the social worker/facilitator for further clarification and deepening of your shared information through in-depth interview.

Appendix B:
ACTIVITY – SELF-NARRATIVE REPORT / ART SYMBOLISM
(TAGALOG INSTRUMENT)

Objectives:

1. Upang makapagpahayag ng sariling pananaw at pagkilanlan sa sarili
2. Upang maibahagi ang sarili ng walang panghuhusga
3. Upang makapagbigay ng impormasyon na maaring magamit upang mas maunawaan ang buhay.
4. Upang mas maintindihan ang mga karanasan sa children in conflict with the law.

Instructions:

1. Siguraduhing kumpleto ang mga materyal bago magsimula tulad ng ballpen,papel at art maerials.
2. Maari ninyong simulan sa isang pagpapakilala (pero hindi tunay na pangalan) o kaya naman mga pananaw nyo sa inyong buhay.
3. Sa inyong papel, maari nyong isulat ang mga bagay tungkol sa inyong karanasan bilang isang CICL.
4. Maari nyong ikwento ang mga karanasan nyo kung bago kayo humantong sa buhay nyo na meron kayo ngayon. Maari din isalaysay ang mga pagbabago pagkatapos ng programa sa loob ng MYRC.
5. Maari nyong ikwento ang mga bagay na nakapagbigay o nakapag-impluwensya sa inyong buhay.
6. Maari nyo din maipahayag ang mga kahilingan nyo para sa gobyerno o ibang ahensiya na makaka pagbigay pa sa inyo ng pagbabago.
7. Sa huling iyong pangungusap, maari nyong ibahagi ang napagtanto (reflection) pagkatapos mo isulat ang iyong mga karanasan.
8. Magdrawing sa isang bondpapaer ng nagsisimbulo ng karanasan mo bilang isang CICL. Isalaysay sa social worker ang personal na interpretasyon ng simbulong naisagawa.
9. Pagkatapos ito isulat, ipasa sa social worker upang mabasa ito at maitanong ang mga bagay para sa paglilinaw na katanungan at in-depth interview.

Appendix C: INFORMED CONSENT

Greetings Former Resident of MYRC!

You are invited to join a phenomenological study entitled "The Second Chance: The Lived Experiences of Former Residents of Manila Youth Reception Center Reintegrated with their Families and Communities. Please take whatever time you need to discuss the study with your family and friends, or anyone else you wish to. The decision to join, or not to join, is up to you. In this study, I will reflectively describe and analyzed the lived experiences of Former Residents of Manila Youth Reception Center Reintegrated with their Families and Communities and explore the possible meanings and insights that may be derived.

If you decide to participate this is a basic outline of what will happen over the course of your participation __________________. We think this will take you ___________. The investigators may stop the study or take you out of the study at any time they judge it is in your best interest. They may also remove you from the study for various other reasons. They can do this without your consent. You can stop participating at any time. If you stop you will not lose any benefits.

This study involves the following risks _________________. There may also be other risks that we cannot predict. It is reasonable to expect the following benefits from this research: ________________________. However, we can't guarantee that you will personally experience benefits from participating in this study. Others may benefit in the future from the information we find in this study.

We will take the following steps to keep information about you confidential, and to protect it from unauthorized disclosure, tampering, or damage: ___________. In some cases it may be necessary, for your safety or for the integrity of the study, for individuals from the MYRC or appointed by the MYRC, institution staff, IRB or sponsor to access your data.

Your information or bio-specimens, even if the identifying information is removed, will not be used or distributed for future research studies The information or bio-specimens collected from you in this research study might be stripped of identifying information and used for other research in the future. If we use the information/specimens in future research studies, or share the information/specimens with other researchers so they can use it, we would first remove anything that would identify you. We would use or share the de-identified information/specimens without getting additional permission (consent) from you.

Participation in this study is voluntary. You have the right not to participate at all or to leave the study at any time. Deciding not to participate or choosing to leave the study will not result in any penalty or loss of benefits to which you are entitled, and it will not harm your relationship with _______________.

Call ____________________ at ___________________ or email___________ at ___________if you have questions about the study, any problems, unexpected physical or psychological discomforts, any injuries, or think that something unusual or unexpected is happening.

Signature of Co-researcher/Representative   Date

________________________________   ____________________

Appendix D: RELATED STUDIES MATRIX

A. FOREIGN STUDIES

Author/s	Objective Of The Study	Territorial Coverage	Results/Edetic Insight	Implications
Christian Ranheim	The report provides statistical and narrative overviews of the juvenile justice situation and systems in all ASEAN countries.	The study has been financed by Swedish Development Cooperation under RWI's Regional Asia Programme, and carried out under the auspices of RWI's office in Jakarta.	Concludes that the number of juveniles below the age of 18 who are deprived of their liberty in ASEAN (Association of Southeast Asian Nations) countries could be reduced significantly if proper alternatives to criminal justice proceedings were applied to their fullest potential.	This study provides statistical and narrative overviews of the juvenile justice situation and systems in all ASEAN countries that I can use to have a macro perspective of interventions and phenomenon of CICL.
			It also finds that a remarkably low number of juveniles are in contact with the formal criminal justice system	
			Statistics on the juvenile justice situation in the region, which show that each year 70,000 children are charged with a criminal offence in ASEAN countries. This is far less than in other comparable parts of the world.	
			The study identifies a number of issues of common concern across member states, and RWI hopes that it may lead to new initiatives and dialogue that may in the future enhance the protection of children in conflict with the law in the ASEAN region.	
UNICEF	the aim to continuously improve transparency and use of evaluation of the Intervention and Rehabilitation Program in Residential Facilities and Diversion Programs for Children in Conflict with the Law	Residential Facilities and Diversion Programs for Children in Conflict with the Law in the Philippines	All of the programs under evaluation are found to be relevant in meeting the needs of CICL in the areas of health care, education, skills, security and safety, and spiritual and value formation.	This study provides significant gaps and current phenomenon of CICL programs and interventions. This study can help me to better understand the phenomenon in a wider scale especially to the existing interventions and programs for CICL.
			They are also relevant to the aim of bringing Philippine juvenile justice law and practice into compliance with international conventions.	
			However, significant gaps still exist in meeting international conventions' rights protection standards.	
			The full implementation of the Law, especially the diversion	

			programs, and adequate compliance at the local level are not satisfactory.	
			Considerable evidence has shown that most programs provide an enabling environment for the rehabilitation and reintegration of CICL. Interviews with parents and children confirm changes in the behavior of the CICL in the programs.	
			As almost all the facilities visited provide same services for CICL under sentence suspension, rehabilitation, intervention, and diversion, this evaluation is not able to articulate the changes brought about by the different programs to CICL.	
			Moreover, official statistics on the percentage of former CICL who go back to school or who find a job are unavailable.	
			There is likewise no available empirical data on the recidivism rate of CICL who have participated in the programs, as compared to those who have not.	

B. LOCAL STUDIES

Authors	Objective Of The Study	Territorial Coverage	Results/Edetic Insight	Implications
Kristine D. Aala, Jenie M. Ramos, Reuben Mendoza, Emerson Magnaye, Merwina Lou A. Bautista.	This study aimed to determine the intervention programs on juvenile delinquency implemented by selected barangay in Batangas City.	The respondents of this research were Brgy. officials of selected barangays in Batangas City.	In terms of Physical and Health, the program that is highly implemented is the Clean and Green Program while for education is the Free Education Program. Program on Material Recovery is perceived by majority of the respondents as highly implemented with respect to livelihood.	This study provides the impact of different intervention program on juvenile delinquency. This study is a very useful for me to be able to understand the impact of different intervention programs towards CICL development Physically, Psychologically, and Spiritually
			In terms of the psychological, spiritual and development of on children in conflict with the law it was found out that parent-child interaction program was the highest.	
			The continuous implementation of the programs is recommended for the effective rehabilitation and restoration of child in conflict with the law.	
			Furthermore utilization and improvement of other programs would also be substantial in developing the character and	

			personality of these children.	
Adhikain Para sa Karapatang Pambata Ateneo Human Rights Center	To conduct research study about the situation of children in conflict with the law	Selected metro manila cities	The diversion procedure is limited in its scope Diversion under the Rules only covers offences where the maximum penalty imposed by law is imprisonment of not more than six months. Diversion under the Rules is limited to cases wherein the complaint or information is filed with the Family Courts. Diversion programme under the Rules may include community-based programmes or work-detail programmes in the community. Under the Rules, the Committee may only recommend diversion if the complainant does not object thereto.	This study provides an understanding and evaluation of the diversion program for CICL. It helps me to understand the gaps and scope and limitations that can be added in further possibilities of my studies.
Marjon Junederbyshire	This thesis investigates and identifies processes of 'spiritual transformation' in rehabilitation programmes for boys from prison in the Philippines.	Data were collected for this qualitative research by means of individual and group interviews and participant and non-participant observation in ten institutions during five weeks fieldwork in the Philippines. Members of staff and resident boys were interviewed in jails and rehabilitation centres and some boys were visited in their homes.	The thesis argues that boys who suffer deprivation at home, on the streets and in jail become alienated from society. When events lead to an experience of spiritual awakening, the subsequent treatment they receive can either lead them to make changes in their lives or it can thwart them from doing so. With encouragement, boys are able to consolidate positive life changes and reach a lasting condition of spiritual transformation. The thesis demonstrates how some programmes of rehabilitation in the Philippines allow deprived children to experience and develop constructive relationships of trust, reliance, attachment and commitment, and how this assists the development of faith that is a significant component of spiritual transformation. The thesis shows how such programmes catalyse and nurture this spiritual transformation.	This study makes an original contribution to knowledge in the area of rehabilitation of Children in Conflict with the Law and the spiritual aspects of rehabilitation. It builds upon previous research in the field of faith development and adds to this body of scholarship. Findings gained from this research can be applied to policy elsewhere.

www.ingramcontent.com/pod-product-compliance
Lightning Source LLC
LaVergne TN
LVHW060822170826
845678LV00010B/1864

* 9 7 8 6 2 1 4 7 0 5 8 8 7 *